Faith and Justice
Living as Christians
on a Small Planet

Faith and Justice
Living as Christians on a Small Planet

by Sister Margaret Betz

Saint Mary's Press
Christian Brothers Publications
Winona, Minnesota

To the students at the Newman Center
of Wayne State University
whose questions prompted this book,
and whose hopes for the future are for justice and peace.

There is no way to thank adequately all of the people who have contributed to this book. I am especially grateful to Robert K. Betz of Fairbanks, Alaska, and to Gerald F. Cavanagh, SJ, of Detroit, Michigan, who, from this book's very conception, offered their encouragement, valuable insights, and helpful criticism. Joseph P. Daoust, SJ, was a great help in clarifying issues, and Ann Guettler Berger, Mary Denek, Frank Hillebrand, Thomas Hinsberg, and Katie White carefully critiqued the manuscript in various phases of preparation.

One year of financial support from the Danforth Foundation provided me with the opportunity to research the issues and to meet with concerned people across the country. In Detroit, the IHM Sisters at Marygrove Convent shared freely of their time, experience, and resources. I thank each of them.

Acknowledgments continue on page 176

Nihil Obstat: Msgr. William T. Magee, PhD
                 Censor Deputatus
                 March 18, 1980
Imprimatur: †Loras J. Watters, DD
                 Bishop of Winona
                 March 18, 1980

Edited by Stephan M. Nagel

ISBN: 0-88489-114-3
Library of Congress Card Catalog Number: 80-50259

Contents

Preface:
Our Journey Toward Justice

Life is a journey. This journey image has fired the imaginations of many people throughout history. From earliest times explorers and pioneers have made exciting, dangerous journeys a part of their lives. We can still relate to journey images since they are very much a part of how we live—from hiking trails to jet travel.

Journeys force questions. Where shall I go? How shall I get there? How long shall I stay? The journey of life forces questions too. Who am I? What is the meaning and purpose of my life? How can I be happy? What is my ultimate destiny? The question can be asked in many ways, but it is the same basic question: What is life all about?

The answer can never be "told"; it can only be discovered. The key to that discovery lies in our willingness to enter fully into our own life journey, to cherish its mystery, and to share its joys and sorrows. It further lies in our ability to recognize that our decisions and actions can be positive forces in enhancing our personal life journeys and in shaping the world around us.

Faith and Justice: Living as Christians on a Small Planet offers both an invitation and a challenge. Its invitation: to look deeply within ourselves to learn how we are both gifted and needy, and to look deeply at the world around us to see how it too is gifted and needy. Its challenge: to make career and lifestyle decisions that enhance those gifts and respond to those needs, and so to move this world toward justice.

When we accept this invitation and challenge we allow the Spirit of God to expand our consciousness, to give us eyes to see in new ways, minds to understand with new depth, and courage to respond more fully to the needs of our age. This is a journey toward justice. It is what our lives and this book are all about.

1

Perspectives:
The Way We See the World

Anyone who wants to save his life will lose it; but anyone who loses his life for my sake, and for the sake of the gospel, will save it.

Mark 8:35

Long before the dawn of human history, this earth was touched by God's life-giving Spirit. Earth became alive and ever so slowly began to produce a wide variety of vegetation and animals, each distinctive and interrelated with other forms of life and with the environment. Even now, some billions of years later, creation continues to evolve and to develop as a marvelous complexity of living things, an interdependent web of life-giving cycles of incredible delicacy and diversity.

1 Evolution and Human Decisions

At some point lost in history, human beings began making conscious decisions which shaped their own lives as well as history itself. Paleontologist Mary Leakey has spent much of her life studying human origins in southeast Africa. Some years ago, she and her co-workers discovered footprints of beings who might well be our remote but direct ancestors. Cast in hardened volcanic ash, this trail of footprints was made more than three and a half million years ago. These prints produced for Mary Leakey what she terms a "time wrench." Leakey recreates the scene as she sees it:

> **At one point, and you need not be an expert tracker to discern this, she [Leakey guesses that the creature was female] stops, pauses, turns to the left to glance at some possible threat or irregularity, and then continues north. This motion, so intensely human, transcends time. Three million six hundred thousand years ago, a remote ancestor—just as you or I—experienced a moment of doubt.**

This moment was also a moment of decision. Although we do not know anything more about that human-like being than the footprints can tell us, this discovery puts us in touch with the historical roots of human decisions. And while we do not know anything about the individuals who first used fire or language, or invented the wheel, or grew grain or domesticated animals, these human decisions made our lives very much what they are today.

From its very beginning the human family has stood neither above nor outside of creation, but within it. Unique in dignity, intelligence, and ability to influence future generations, we have been given the capacity to grace this Earth with new heights of beauty, loveliness, and creativity. Like our ancestors of long ago we have the imagination to dream and to fantasize and to form mental pictures of situations that we have not actually experienced. To a degree undreamed of by those same ancestors, we have the expertise or engineering skills to make our dreams become reality by putting power and materials to work for people. This combination of imagination and engineering skills— "imagineering"—can be a dynamic tool for making decisions that creatively and effectively shape our immediate environment and our future.

Imagineering is that wonderfully human capacity to learn from the past, to deal with the present, and to shape the future. It unites human imagination and technological bent into a vital force of creative energy. On a personal level, imagineering impels us to live creatively and conscientiously to become all that we are capable of becoming. On a social level, imagineering drives us to examine our lives and our world, to fantasize alternative possibilities, and to direct society's institutions toward those possibilities by the skillful use of talents. By imagineering we bring human values, technological competence, and a world perspective to bear on our personal decisions.

All people make decisions. The decisions of individual men and women have changed not only their own lives, but the direction of history itself. Those decisions may not seem very important at times, but their impact can be profound. This impact is illustrated in the following examples:

At the turn of the century, a young man set out to make his dream a reality. Spurred on by the idea that every man should own an automobile, Henry Ford mass-produced the Model T and sold it at a price the average person could afford. His decision changed the course of history.

Although scientists had known about the structure of the atom since the early 1900s, forty-odd years passed before they were able to produce the first man-made chain reaction. With that event, for good or ill, Italian physicist Enrico Fermi and his colleagues inaugurated the nuclear age and changed the course of history.

For centuries before the mid-1950s, the paralytic polio virus had crippled hundreds of thousands of people, many of them children. After years of laborious research, Dr. Jonas Salk, an American physician, developed a vaccine that effectively reduced the incidence of polio in the United States by nearly ninety-six percent. His decision and dedicated work in service to humanity changed the course of history.

On December 1, 1955, a weary black seamstress in Montgomery, Alabama, refused to give up her bus seat to a white passenger. Her arrest sparked a new beginning in the civil rights movement. People took courage and followed in her steps. Although many never knew her name, Rosa Parks's decision changed the course of history.

In the early sixties, a meticulous scientist and writer

stunned the world with the terrifying revelation of how human carelessness, greed, and irresponsibility were contaminating the Earth. For some years her message fell on deaf ears. Now "ecology" is a household word and the care of the Earth a growing concern. Rachel Carson and her book, *Silent Spring*, changed the course of history.

In 1967, a final decision was made to eradicate smallpox. Under the auspices of the World Health Organization and the leadership of Dr. Donald Henderson, search teams fanned out across Africa, South America, and every corner of the globe where outbreaks had been recorded. After years of sustained commitment by many individuals, that decision too has changed the course of history.

Our decisions count. Our actions count. Even if we do not know what the long-range consequences of our actions might be, nevertheless history is shaped and sometimes radically changed by our decisions. One philosopher put it this way: in fashioning ourselves, we fashion humanity.

2 Our Fundamental Perspective

Each of us has a way of looking at the world that captures something of its overall plan, but few of us have so expansive a vision that we capture sufficiently its mystery and its reality. Still our fundamental perspective — the way each of us sees the world and ourselves in it — is an essential key to our decision-making. Whether narrow or wide, whether optimistic or pessimistic, our fundamental perspective dominates all our views and shapes our major decisions. Ask yourself: How might a student see the world differently than a miner? How might a taxi driver see it differently than a jet pilot? How might a Manhattan

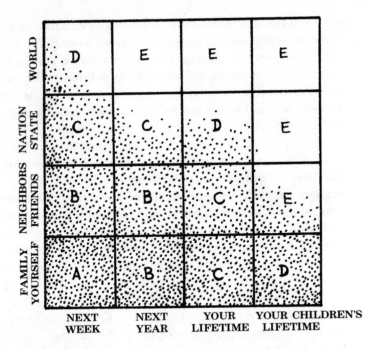

EXPANDING PERSPECTIVES. This figure shows how our decisions can be "charted to include more people and a wider time span."

banker see it differently than a Kenyan villager? Each of these people makes decisions based on their fundamental perspective. This is true even when they do not recognize this fact.

The most important change we can make is to expand our way of looking at the world. Such a change could be sudden and profound. More often it is gradual. As we change our way of looking at the world, we change our way of being and acting. The figure above shows how we can change our way of looking at the world by expanding our perspective. Can you think of examples of decisions we might make in the clusters marked A, B, C, D, and E? For this exercise, limit your examples by looking only for the *foreseeable effects* of our decisions.

When we make decisions regarding the daily necessities of life with little thought beyond our immediate concerns, our vision is limited and narrow. These decisions are not necessarily good or bad, but they can take on new meaning as we expand our way of looking at the world.

Some decisions demonstrate our concern for the world beyond immediate personal or family needs. When we are active in a block club, a hospital guild, a food cooperative, a political party, or any group or institution that is trying to improve the quality of life, we act out of a wider and better perspective. We make decisions that have an impact on people beyond ourselves and our immediate families. Some decisions look to the long-term good of people we do not know, people of other cultures and languages, people living now and those in future generations. All of our decisions stem from our fundamental perspective.

3 Four Limited Perspectives

No one can "give" another person a fundamental perspective. Family, friends, and teachers contribute to its development, but formulating a perspective about the world is the task of each person growing toward maturity. This world view includes a way of seeing self, others, the world, and history in terms of time and space. We can discover our world view by examining the way we look at ourselves, the way we think of history, and the way we treat others, that is, our sense of justice. We can expand that world view as we understand more deeply how our decisions affect ourselves, our history, and others.

Four limited world views and their implications for personal decisions are described below. These are not exhaustive, clear-cut views of the world. They are abstractions. None of them adequately describes any person. At times elements of the **spectator, conformist, isolationist,** and **profiteer** exist in all of us, even when we do not use those labels or recognize that fact. The common thread tying these views together is the boundaries or limitations with which each of them narrows our perspective and influences our decision-making.

PERSPECTIVE 1: SPECTATORS

Sometimes we feel ill-prepared to cope with life or we feel powerless to change ourselves or our situation. When we feel helpless, we sometimes refuse to make decisions. Instead we allow other people and circumstances to shape our lives more than is necessary. When powerlessness dominates our lives, we live in a rut of non-decision. Since we do not believe our actions can make any difference, we act as if nothing matters—or as if nothing "on earth" matters. We act as **spectators.**

Spectators have decided that the present situation is too complicated and messy. Because the present seems meaningless to the spectator, the past and future sometimes take on a rosy glow. History can become a romantic fable about how marvelous the world once was. And the future can be filled with an image of heaven which ignores the present altogether. Believing that wrongdoing will be corrected in the life-to-come, spectators are not inclined to get involved in righting injustice. "Justice" is a dream postponed until the Last Judgment.

PERSPECTIVE 2: CONFORMISTS

Because we sometimes find that the world is unreliable and unpredictable, we adopt plans or join groups which we hope will protect us from dangers and threats. We act as **conformists** when we use these plans not only to shape history but to control it *entirely.* When feelings of insecurity dominate our lives, we try to strip history of its mystery.

Conformists put history on a reliable, predictable basis. They reduce all the lessons of history down to one. It is that those who have "the right stuff"—knowledge, character, attitudes, background—are rewarded by prosperity. On the other hand, those who have suffered or failed must have done something wrong. As a result, conformists value people, not as mysteries, but in terms of how *useful* or *valuable* they are to their plans. Parents act as conformists when they pressure sons or daughters to succeed academically in order to "insure" their future success. Peers act as conformists when they mistreat those who are not "with it," not conforming to group standards regarding dress, drugs, or attitudes.

Justice, for the conformist, is spelled "just us." It is reserved for those in "our" group and it is defined by "our" rules. In the conformist's world view, "losers"—that is, the poor, the weak, and the dissenters—are given no thought at all.

PERSPECTIVE 3: ISOLATIONISTS

Sometimes we feel frustrated or defeated by the demands of our families or communities. In an attempt to be free, we ignore or protest our duties to them. When irresponsible freedom dominates our lives, we act as **isolationists.**

Isolationists believe that people should do "their own thing" because these are acts of freedom. Decision-making itself is seen by isolationists as freedom without accompanying responsibility. Our TV westerns and detective shows are filled with characters who can make the "tough choices" just a little faster than those they kill, and who ride off into the sunset leaving misery and grief behind.

History is meaningless for isolationists because it burdens them and restricts their freedom. Isolationists believe they must make their decisions alone. Neither memory nor hopes should intrude upon the powerful moment of decision.

Isolationists are as strongly opposed to group endeavors as conformists are in favor of them. Groups with long experience and professionals and experts hold no interest for them. Even groups that contribute in some way to the health and growth of their members cannot win their support. "Justice" is limited to the isolationist's personal triumph over another person or group.

PERSPECTIVE 4: PROFITEERS

When profiteering dominates our lives, our major concern is

"taking care of Number One." Any time we are willing to manipulate others for our advantage without regard for their welfare, we act as **profiteers.** Imagine a high school coach who forces an injured player to play out the "big game." Imagine a person who dates only the "big names" at school. Or imagine the "big name" who makes dates "earn" the privilege by putting out sexually.

History is filled with activities of profiteers, mainly as some form of slavery—frequently toward women, children, foreigners, or the poor. The profiteer has no interest in the lessons of history except those that offer power or advantage. The profiteer, for instance, is willing to protect and promote oppressive institutions and traditions which keep women "in their place," foreigners out of the marketplace, and the poor hungry enough to take tedious, low-paying jobs. "Justice," to the profiteer, is at best a sentimental brand of charity, aimed at earning some self-satisfaction.

4 Two Calamities

As mentioned earlier, no one works solely out of any of these perspectives. Nor are these the only four views that could be described. More important is the fact that when people are compelled to make decisions and especially when people are too anxious or pressured, they find themselves acting out of limited perspectives which are too narrow or distorted, like the ones above. The following examples point out how warped or shriveled world views can affect our decisions in utterly disastrous ways.

CHIEF LUTHER STANDING BEAR

In the last two centuries, the United States has paid scant respect and attention to the needs and welfare of native Americans. Settlers were often in a great rush to establish their own brands of progress and religion on this continent. As a result, many American Indian tribes were destroyed, rich cultures were lost, and those that survived were left in confusion and poverty.

Long ago Chief Luther Standing Bear reflected sadly upon the difference between what he described as the Indian and white viewpoints:

> **We do not think of the great open plains, the beautiful hills, and the winding streams with tangled growth as "wild." Only to the white man was nature a "wilderness" and was the land "infested" with "wild" animals and "savage" people.**

In the settlers' view, these hundreds of different tribes, with their rich and varied traditions, were simply an obstacle to fulfilling "progress" or "destiny" in America.

COMMANDANT RUDOLF HOESS

Commandant Rudolf Hoess, the second example (drawn from William Styron's book *Sophie's Choice*), involves one of many tormenting questions still asked about the millions of murders committed during World War II at Auschwitz and other death camps in Europe. The question is this: How could people commit and witness endless murder without feeling at least simple pity for the suffering of so many others? The philosopher Hannah Arendt suggests that "the trick" was to turn that pity inward: "So that instead of saying 'What horrible things I did to people!' the murderers would be able to say, 'What horrible things I had to watch. . .!'" The testimony of Rudolf Hoess, the commander of Auschwitz, reveals precisely this stifling sort of self-pitying view toward his outrages:

> **I had to see everything . . . I had to watch hour after hour. I had to stand for hours on end in the ghastly stench . . . I had to look through the peephole of the gas chambers and watch the process of death itself.**

These statements by Chief Luther Standing Bear and Commandant Hoess not only help us to see how our fundamental perspective affects our behavior, but also hint at how our perspective contains our self-image. Curiously, Chief Luther Standing Bear, with his tribe a victim of white oppression, left behind words filled with dignity and conviction. His belief in and love for all the created world allowed him a clear understanding of the injustice of white settlers. Hoess, on the other hand, exercised nearly absolute power over the lives of millions of people. Yet amazingly his words suggest that he, not the millions, was the victim.

Both of these calamities suggest two crucial guidelines for developing our fundamental perspective.

> **1) Our perspective should confirm within us the great value of ourselves as persons as well as the ultimate value of human life itself.**

> **2) Our perspective should compel us to look beyond our own needs to recognize the needs of others as well.**

In the next section we will see how a religious perspective fulfills these two basic requirements and provides a truly human world view.

5 The Religious Sense

In all of the perspectives and cases just described, religious questions are hidden. Each of these perspectives proposes tentative answers to the ultimate questions men and women have struggled with throughout history:

Who am I? What is the meaning and purpose of life? What is goodness and what is evil? Where is true happiness to be found? Why is there suffering? What is death? What does it mean to be human?

At the heart of these questions lies the mystery of person, and the mystery of the relationship of persons with one another and,

ultimately, with a Power and Reality greater than ourselves. The answers can never be fully explained, the mystery never fully grasped, but eventually we come to believe what we feel is the truth about these mysteries.

Our deeply rooted religious sense is the thrust of the human spirit toward some incomprehensible fulfillment, toward some unknown, more vibrant destiny. There has never been a tribe or culture of people that did not cherish a belief in the "beyond" and engage in some kind of worship. This religious sense continues in our day to be a powerful force in shaping the lives of individuals and in shaping history itself. While other human traits—creating tools, learning language, building culture—are important, the outstanding characteristic of the human family throughout history has been its religious strivings. This is because religion offers the widest possible framework for dealing with life's toughest questions.

Further, while we can try to ignore our religious sense, we cannot deny it some form of expression. In Marxist countries where governments have tried to replace a religious framework with secular values, for example, attempts have failed. Eventually we believe because we cannot *not* believe in something. The writer G. K. Chesterton once said that he could not be an atheist because it would take too much faith. For the atheist, faith is the belief that there is no God. The current upswing in new religious cults and of some stifling, fanatic forms of religion further suggests that we must come to terms with our religious sense rather than ignore the need for meaning, security, and hope that it includes.

This religious sense finds expression in ways that are both authentic and inauthentic. When we express our religious sense in an authentic manner we realize its power to discover life's ultimate meaning and to create new possibilities. We sense unity with the whole human family and with God who made us all. This in turn prompts us to works of love and service.

When we express that same religious sense in an inauthentic manner, however, we restrict its life-giving power and bind our-

Dorothy Day
Journalist and Publisher

Since 1917 when she was arrested for picketing on behalf of women's suffrage, Dorothy Day has been in the forefront of causes ranging from civil rights to disarmament to prison reform. For almost fifty years she has been the inspiration and backbone of a movement which combines a life of simplicity with active concern for people, especially those suffering from hunger, poverty, violence, and discrimination.

Dorothy's life direction began to take shape during her college days. As a student at the University of Illinois in Urbana she often went to Chicago where she witnessed the plight of people burdened by social problems. Efforts to change that plight led her to join the Socialist Party and later the International Workers of the World. She began her career in journalism by writing for their publications.

After two years at the University of Illinois, Dorothy moved with her family to New York City. Her father objected to a woman in journalism, so she left home and took a succession of newspaper jobs with radical groups.

In 1932, while the country was experiencing the great depression, Dorothy was experiencing a great inner conversion. Her baptism into the Catholic faith deepened her desire to help people on the fringes of society. The question was, "How?" The answer began to crystalize later that year when Dorothy Day met Peter Maurin. Dorothy found the companionship and challenge in him that she needed to put her new-found faith into practice. Together they began the Catholic Worker Movement: houses of hospitality where the down-and-out can come for food and shelter, farming communes where people can live in voluntary simplicity, and a monthly tabloid that tells of life as it is and prods people to respond with caring and effective decisions.

During all the years that Dorothy has struggled for justice she has not allowed herself to be crushed by the despair all around her. Her face is lined with years of struggle, but her eyes are illuminated by the power of love within.

selves to trite and manipulative ways. Instead of love and service, we are overly concerned with self and tend to ignore the needs of those around us. Thus, in every believer at one time or another, we find some evidence of the limited perspectives like the ones described above.

> We make *spectating* a part of our religion when we use religion as an excuse to avoid making decisions altogether.

> We make *conforming* a part of our religion when we make idols out of human endeavors.

> We make *isolationism* a part of our religion when we believe that we can have a "God and me" relationship without regard for other people.

> We make *profiteering* a part of our religion when we make idols out of things and slaves out of people.

Obviously, by making these limited perspectives a part of our religion, we distort our religious sense and narrow the perspective that it offers.

6 The Christian Perspective and Justice

Central to all the major religions of the world is belief in (1) a deity or deities who enter into vital relationship with human beings, (2) a body of accepted teaching or doctrine, and (3) a code of ethics.

Every religion deals with many of the same issues—meaning, death, happiness, evil, immortality. Often what distinguishes one particular religion from another is the kind of deity its adherents believe in. Each provides a particular religious perspective based on someone's unique experience and understanding. The followers of Jesus accept his understanding of God as Father and his resurrection as reported by his disciples. This unique religious perspective provides us with a clear response to the questions raised by our religious sense.

The Hebrew Scripture reveals a God who is close to his people. His active presence among them is among the oldest and most enduring of biblical promises. Moreover, the Hebrew Scripture is very explicit about the close relationship between Yahweh, the God of Israel, and one's neighbor. "This is what Yahweh asks of you: only this, to act justly, to love tenderly, and to walk humbly with your God" (Micah 6:8). To know Yahweh is to do justice to one's neighbor, to do justice to one's neighbor is to be known by Yahweh. This is the essential message of the great Hebrew prophets, especially Isaiah, Jeremiah, and Hosea. Yahweh is a God of justice and compassion. The only appropriate human response to his presence is in decisions and actions based in compassion and justice. "Take your wrongdoing out of my sight. Cease to do evil. Learn to do good, search for justice, help the oppressed, be just to the orphan, plead for the widow" (Isaiah 1:16-17).

Christians recognize this God of compassion in the life and words of Jesus, the carpenter from Nazareth. Yahweh's presence and concern for the poor, the widow, the orphan, and for all who live on the fringes of society is "enfleshed" in that simple man who described his mission in the words of the prophet Isaiah:

The spirit of the Lord Yahweh has been given to me, for Yahweh has anointed me. He has sent me to bring good news to the poor, to bind up the hearts that are broken, to proclaim liberty to captives, freedom to those in prison . . . (Isaiah 61:1).

As we come to recognize ever more deeply the God of compassion in Jesus, we open ourselves to a conversion or change of heart. This change of heart is an experience of God which expands and deepens our fundamental perspective so that we can see with new eyes, understand with new minds, and turn our energies to new ways of living.

Thus what was revealed in the Hebrew Scripture is given even

Martin Luther King, Jr.
Clergyman and Civil Rights Leader
Awarded Nobel Peace Prize—1964

When Martin Luther King, Jr., was killed by an assassin's bullet early in the evening of April 4, 1968, he left a legacy of love and hope to a nation torn by anger and despair. For thirteen years, this unpretentious man from a middle-class Georgia family had been a bridge between the frustation of black people and the unconcern of white people. Those efforts cost him his life.

At twenty-six, King was finishing his dissertation for a doctorate from Boston University and was pastor of Dexter Avenue Baptist Church in Montgomery, Alabama. Suddenly he was catapulted into the leadership of a movement that would bring new freedom to black people and would change every institution across this country. It began so simply. Rosa Parks, a black woman, refused to give her seat on the bus to the white man who demanded it. Her decision and subsequent arrest was the straw that broke the camel's back. Montgomery's clergymen organized a boycott of the city's buses and chose King to lead it. For over a year black people either walked or used the clergy-operated car and taxi pool.

Montgomery was only the beginning. In Birmingham and Selma, in Chicago and Washington, D.C., King led hundreds, then hundreds of thousands of people in acts of civil disobedience to effect civil rights. Their astonishing self-discipline and nonviolence in the face of mortal danger is a tribute to this man who based his program of nonviolence on the teaching of Jesus, the social ideas of Henry Thoreau, and the methods of Mohandas Gandhi.

In December 1964, Martin Luther King went to Oslo, Norway, to accept the Nobel Peace Prize. On that occasion he reiterated his message: "Nonviolence is the answer to the crucial political and moral question of our day—the need for man to overcome oppression and violence without resorting to violence and oppression." King never wavered in that conviction. To the very end, he was the revolutionist armed only with love.

greater scope in the New Testament: to know the Father is to do the works of justice to all people; to do the works of justice to all people is to be known by the Father. The idea of "neighbor" is extended beyond the boundaries of race or country. The only appropriate human response to the mystery of Jesus—our faith—is in compassionate decisions and actions *on as wide a scale as possible.*

This was a creative, revolutionary change in the notion of justice. Never before was justice seen as the right of every individual regardless of race, sex, social status, or wealth. The God of Jesus was very difficult for people to accept partly because his love embraced all people and condemned the practice of every kind of slavery. Slavery, perhaps the most blatant example of social injustice, goes back to ancient times. Slaves frequently worked without pay, had no legal right to marry or have a family, to testify in court, or to own property. Primarily an economic institution, slavery also penetrated the world's political, cultural, and religious institutions. Today, while few nations legally allow slavery, its effects continue to pervade social policy. Like the slaves of earlier times, some people today are forced to live on the fringes of society, victims of injustice, owned by those who own everything they need to live.

This revolutionary view of justice which Jesus revealed so frightened the world at that place and time that there were vigorous attempts to destroy early Christianity. In fact, so difficult was this truth to accept that many centuries passed before the human rights implied by his truth were recognized in Puritan America and in the French Revolution.

While some might feel that this delay—this long infancy—implies the impracticality of Jesus' vision, it is just as fair to say that it suggests the irresistible power of his truth and the relentlessness of God's love. Jesus' belief in the worth of the individual is something we sense in ourselves. Nevertheless, there is much in human history and society which denies the worth of "certain" other people. This powerful presence of evil in human life is reflected in the term Christians give to it: original sin.

Since Vatican II, Catholics are coming to a deepened understanding of the meaning and importance of justice. In 1971, the Synod of Bishops stated in *Justice in the World:*

Action on behalf of justice and participation in the transformation of the world fully appear to us as a constitutive dimension of the preaching of the Gospel, or in other words of the Church's mission for the redemption of the human race and its liberation from every oppressive situation (#6).

As we face the urgent problems of our world and ask questions and seek answers and study options, we must weigh the alternatives from the perspective of the Christian gospel of compassion. As Christian people, we are coming to understand more fully that God has chosen to create men and women as makers of human history, with full and inherent freedom in our individual and collective destiny. *We are coming to realize that Jesus' challenge to us is to become more fully human ourselves by sharing and shaping human history with others.*

7 Justice and Growth

Justice has its roots in the value we place on human life. When we see ourselves as lovable persons in relationship with others who also require and deserve love, we are growing in justice. Justice means that each person has the opportunity to achieve his or her full human potential and the duty to provide that same basic opportunity for others.

No one is born just, however. Children have the potential for relationships and responsibility and therefore for justice, but it takes many years of gentle and challenging education to become a just person. Youth and adults have relationships and responsibilities, but even among friends and neighbors, we are not always just. In other words, we find it difficult to achieve our own potential and desires; it is even more difficult to work to provide these opportunities for others.

Cesar Chavez has been recognized as a man of justice. For many years a few wealthy landowners controlled much of the agricultural land in California. Farm workers were drawn from people judged too poor to protest—Chicanos, Filipinos, Chinese, Japanese—and were systematically excluded from laws that governed child education and labor. Poverty forced entire families to join the stream of migrant workers who pulled beets, picked grapes, lettuce, and cotton for wealthy growers. Poor, exploited, and unorganized, farm workers seemed to have no recourse to justice. Then, in the mid-sixties, Cesar Chavez, himself a farm worker, organized fellow workers to strike for union recognition. From the beginning, Chavez based

Thomas Gumbleton
Bishop

When Thomas Gumbleton was named auxiliary bishop in Detroit in 1968 at the age of 38, he was the youngest of 300 bishops in the United States. Less than ten years later he was recognized as one of this country's most articulate advocates *against* war and *for* the world's hungry people. Poverty programs, civil rights, questions of peace and war, rights of the oppressed—all won his active support and daily energies.

At Gumbleton's initiative the National Conference of Catholic Bishops issued their strong 1971 anti-war statement even while war dragged on in Indochina. That statement paved the way for a modified return to the understanding of the first three centuries of Christianity when nonviolence was a basic belief.

Gumbleton's outspoken views against the tragedy of war and the arms race go hand in hand with his plea for the world's hungry. "We can't be spending $400 billion per year in the world on arms and, at the same time, providing the people of the world with proper food." From its very beginning, Gumbleton was part of Bread for the World, the Christian citizens' lobby that worked successfully in 1976 to make the Right to Food a foundation of U. S. foreign policy. Later as its president he continued to jab at the collective conscience of America on behalf of hungry people everywhere.

Tom Gumbleton, Bishop, is a remarkably warm and compassionate man. Despite the heavy demands of overseeing nearly ninety parishes in the archdiocese's western region, he knows many people in those parishes on a first name basis and is never too busy when one of them is in need. Known as "Gump" to those close to him, Tom Gumbleton is a true pastor—a "people's person."

his decisions and actions on his personal commitment to non-violence and insisted that union members do the same. Disciplined non-violence, he said, was their road to justice. The struggle was hard, but in 1975, California lawmakers guaranteed the right of agricultural workers to vote for the union of their choice. Disparity between growers and workers lessened and full human life for people in both groups became a more real possibility.

As our fundamental perspective—our world view—expands, gradually our way of living changes too. When our perspective is hopeful and caring, we tend to find ways of living creatively with others. Conversely, when we have a dour, morbid perspective, we tend to do things to make the world seem all the sadder to us. Friendships go undiscovered or unrepaired. Tasks seem impossible. Obstacles sap our hope and will power.

When we see the world in the way Jesus saw it, however, we take on a new, exciting perspective—the one proclaimed in the Sermon on the Mount. Jesus' vision is a challenge which has held a powerful, unceasing grip on the imagination of millions for almost two thousand years.

Instead of spectating, Christians are challenged to confront with hope and imagination the misery, evil, and confusion in the world, continuing to believe that since God lives in history, there is even more grace than sin.

Instead of conforming, Christians are challenged to overthrow any human plan that prevents people from enjoying community, to take risks for justice, freedom, and peace, motivated by the conviction that God's coming Kingdom needs all these treasures.

Instead of isolationism, Christians are challenged to reach out beyond the boundaries of self-interest and self-centeredness to help improve the conditions of suffering people and to restore friendship when it fails. This is the greatest commandment: to love.

Instead of profiteering, Christians are challenged to treat other people graciously, with compassion and care, regardless of the disadvantage or "cost."

The Christian journey toward justice is a difficult challenge. Yet it is a journey to become more fully human, more fully alive to ourselves and to others. The next chapter discusses human talents, needs and values since these are the clues to discovering what being human is all about.

REVIEW QUESTIONS

1) What is significant about the footprints discovered by Mary Leakey and her co-workers?

2) What kinds of decisions broaden our world view or fundamental perspective?

3) What do the four limited perspectives — the spectator, the conformist, the isolationist, and the profiteer— have in common?

4) What two guidelines for developing a personal perspective are suggested by the calamities of Auschwitz and American Indians?

5) In what way is our "religious sense" a powerful force in shaping our lives as individuals and in creating history?

6) What is the essential message of the Hebrew prophets as it relates to justice? How is this view affirmed in Jesus?

7) What is meant by undergoing a "conversion" or change of heart? How does this happen?

8) How would you describe the Christian perspective on life?

2

Talents, Needs, and Values:
Beginning Where You Are

You imagine what you desire;
you will what you imagine;
and at last
you create what you will.
George Bernard Shaw

Our journey to become more fully human is rooted in our past influences and experiences—our life history. Not all of these events have been positive ones for us. Nevertheless by staying in touch with our personal history we can learn more about our fundamental perspective. Gradually we can learn more about the powerful mysteries of being alive, of being a human being, and of being in relationship with others.

The writer George Bernard Shaw effectively integrated his life experiences and history into a thrust toward justice. The theater was his platform for expounding social ideas and generating social reform. Through an intriguing use of comedy, Shaw confronted his audience with the major social problems of his day: exploitation of the poor by slum landlords, exploitation of women by organizers of prostitution, and apathy of the human race as it submitted unquestioningly to modern science.

Shaw described his fundamental perspective simply: ". . . my life belongs to the whole community, and as long as I live it is my privilege to do for it whatsoever I can . . . (Life) is a sort of splendid torch which I have got hold of for the moment, and I want to make it burn as brightly as possible before handing it over to future generations." Future generations, he hoped, would channel their energies toward justice in a broader time and space framework than had his contemporaries. Shaw died in 1950. His challenge stands.

1 Personal Building Blocks

We are each a unique blend of strength and weakness, of inner beauty and false front, of surprising abilities and nagging limitations. Seeing only the weakness and the limitations can discourage us. Seeing only the abilities and the beauty can make us self-centered. We need to develop our talents, to learn about our limitations, to share our inner beauty, and to make our actions a clear reflection of how we feel and of what we value. By searching out our motives we learn to know ourselves, and we are better able to direct our decisions. Three aspects of our inner selves greatly influence our perspective and decisions: personal talents, needs, and values.

TALENTS

It is like a man on his way abroad who summoned his servants and entrusted his property to them. To one he gave five talents, to another two, to a third one; each in proportion to his ability. Then he set out. The man who had received the five talents promptly went and traded with them and made five more. The man who had received two made two more in the same way. But the man who had received one went off and dug a hole in the ground and hid his master's money. Now a long time after, the master of those servants came back and went through his accounts with them. The man who had received the five talents came forward bringing five more. "Sir," he said, "you entrusted me with five talents; here are five more that I have made." His master said to him, "Well done, good and faithful servant; you have shown you can be faithful in small things, I will trust you with greater; come and join in your master's happiness." Next the man with the two talents came forward. "Sir," he said, "you entrusted me with two talents; here are two more that I have made." His master said to him, "Well done, good and faithful servant; you have shown you can be faithful in small things, I will trust you with greater; come and join in your master's happiness." Last came forward the man who had the one talent. "Sir," said he, "I had heard you were a hard man, reaping where you have not sown and gathering where you have not scattered; so I was afraid, and I went off and hid your talent in the ground. Here it is; it was yours, you have it back." But his master answered him, "You wicked and lazy servant! So you knew that I reap where I have not sown and gather where I have not scattered? Well, then, you should have deposited my money with bankers, and on my return I would have recovered my capital with interest. So now, take the talent from him and give it to the man who has the five talents. For to everyone who has will be given more, and he will have more than enough; but from the man who has not, even what he has will be taken away. As for this good-for-nothing servant, throw him out into the dark, where there will be weeping and grinding of teeth" (Matthew 25:14-30).

We might ask ourselves why this man was treated so harshly. Actually, it had nothing to do with the fact that he had only one talent. Rather his downfall was that he refused to use what he had been given. He refused to accept the trust placed in him, to take responsibility for his gift, and to share it with others. His fundamental perspective was narrow, and his decisions inadequate to the responsibility entrusted to him. He was one of history's spectators.

This story reveals several important facts that are particularly pertinent to us as decision makers.

    1) **Each of us receives talents.**
    2) **We differ in the talents we receive.**
    3) **Each of us is responsible for the development and use of whatever talents we are given.**

Pete Seeger
Folk Singer, Author, Composer

Pete Seeger was sixteen years old in the summer of 1935. That was when his father took him from his home in New York City to the Folk Festival in Asheville, North Carolina. There Pete first heard the music of those whom he affectionately calls the "common people." There he experienced a side of America he had never known. From the very beginning, young Seeger liked it.

Seeger went to Harvard for two years, then decided to try his hand at journalism. But it was 1938 and times were hard. Many people were unemployed, Seeger included. Then one day a teacher offered to pay Pete if he would sing for her students. Until then he had never taken money for what was always fun, nor had it occurred to him to make music his career. That request, however, was the beginning . . .

One thing led to another and before long Pete Seeger's musical career was in full swing. Plucking his five string banjo, he spun out stories that he had learned from a variety of people: copper miners in Montana, steel workers in Pittsburgh, even prison inmates in Texas. One man described these stories as hard-hitting songs for hard-hit people.

Singing became Seeger's way to comment on present-day problems, hopes, dreams, and troubles. "Some songs," he wrote, "mainly help people forget their troubles. Other songs help people to understand their troubles. Some few songs inspire people to do something about their troubles." Singing has been Seeger's way to inspire people to *do* something about their troubles. "If I Had a Hammer" is one of his most familiar songs. Its tune is haunting; its words challenging.

When he is not singing, Pete Seeger finds time to work on some of the troubles he sings about. One of his projects was helping to clean up the polluted Hudson River. Seeger is extraordinary as a musician and as a man concerned about all God's creatures: as he puts it, "Fur, fins, or feathers, we're all in this together."

Talents are personal gifts. Developed, they become skills or abilities. Some people mistakenly limit talents to hobbylike activities or to music and art. How many times have we heard people say—or even said ourselves—"Oh, I can't draw or paint; I can't sing or play an instrument. I'm just not talented." That is a narrow view of talent. We can grow beyond it. In reality, each of us has more talents than we will probably discover or use in our entire lifetime. Part of the excitement and challenge of life lies in discovering and developing our talents and in encouraging others to develop theirs. One of the great satisfactions of parents, for instance, is helping their children to discover and to develop their abilities. One of the great satisfactions of teachers is helping students to develop their minds.

Even those who at first seem least gifted often have talents they do not recognize.

Helen Keller is a classic example. Because of a serious illness, she lost both sight and hearing before she was two years old. It would have been so easy—and tragic—for her gifts to have gone untapped. Thanks to the creative ingenuity of her teacher, Anne Sullivan, however, Helen learned to write and then to speak. She graduated from college with honors and went on to help thousands of other handicapped persons live fuller lives and to encourage all people with her strength. Further, while Anne helped Helen to discover her talents, just as surely Helen encouraged and helped to develop Anne's.

One way to recognize our talents is to look at our successes. Probably we are specially gifted in areas where we have succeeded. For example, we may have a talent for self-expression, for listening to people, for persuading others, or for working well under pressure. We may have a talent for solving problems creatively, or for leading and enabling others. We may excel in math, history, science, business, or other academic fields. Even a small success can be important because success is one way to discover our talents. Success can also spur us to begin new projects and to discover other talents.

To learn what our talents are, we must be open to opportunities to discover them.

Many people remember Alexander Graham Bell as the inventor of the telephone, but his primary career and talent was teaching the deaf. The tedious experiments that led to the invention of the telephone were carried on at night and in off hours. After making his mark as a teacher of the deaf, he invented the telephone and continued to live creatively and productively for another forty-five years.

Those who want to make wise decisions will continue to discover their talents throughout life. A talent which is unsuspected at twenty might begin to surface at thirty, and what is only hinted at at thirty might be flourishing by forty. Lived fully, life is like that.

NEEDS

Personal needs are underlying, powerful forces in defining what it means to be fully human. When they are not filled, needs can thwart the development of our talents and potential, and when they are filled, they can urge us to great heights of achievement and love. No one can fill these needs alone. We need others in order to have our own personal needs met and to help others to meet theirs.

Abraham H. Maslow, a noted American psychologist, classified human needs into five categories in ascending levels of importance:

1) *Physiological needs:* **the need for food, water, air, and rest necessary to maintain the body in equilibrium.**

2) *Safety needs:* the need for security, stability, and protection, for freedom from fear and anxiety.

3) *Belongingness and love needs:* the need for giving and receiving affection from people in general, and for having a respected place in our own group.

4) *Esteem needs:* the desire for self-respect, strength, achievement, independence and freedom, as well as the desire for respect and esteem from other people.

5) *Needs for self-actualization:* the desire for self-fulfillment, for becoming everything that we are capable of becoming in the broadest time and space framework.

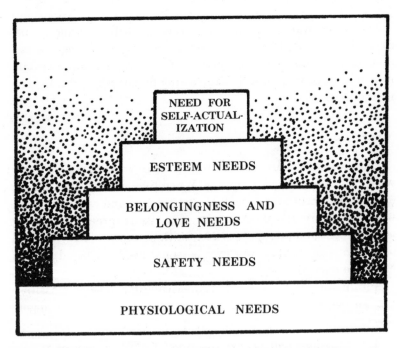

MASLOW'S HIERARCHY OF HUMAN NEEDS. This figure illustrates five categories of human needs. As "lower" needs are met, "higher" needs become more dominant.

This last category of needs for self-actualization is further refined by our religious perspective as Christians: *God has chosen to create us makers of human history with full and inherent freedom in our individual and collective destiny.*

Ordinarily we do not grow in a rigid way but gradually and with needs overlapping. The pattern differs with individuals, but ordinarily as needs at one level are more or less satisfied, needs at the next level become dominant motivating forces. If our needs for safety or security are not met as children, for example, we search for that stability later on in life. Again, people whose only home is the street, whose clothes are rags, and whose daily concern is to get enough to eat have little time or energy for "higher" needs. They are too busy trying to stay alive to be concerned with achieving esteem in the eyes of other people. For them the romantic notion regarding the simple virtues of the poor finds little foothold in reality.

On the other hand, when "lower" needs are met, men and women are able to address their needs for self-actualization, to live and make decisions in a broader time and space framework. They can be concerned with issues that affect more people over a longer time span. Mohandas Gandhi of India, Dag Hammarskjöld of Sweden, and Martin Luther King, Jr. of the United States are examples of people whose hope-filled fundamental perspective led to decisions and efforts in service to humanity.

As we move along to each new step, we increase our capacity to help others, to be more concerned for those whose basic needs are not satisfied. Our decisions, especially major decisions, begin to reflect that concern.

Madeleine Longpre is a dynamic woman and an effective decision maker. In her late thirties, Madeleine's primary career is wife and mother. Consequently, many of her day-to-day decisions center around her husband and their three children. But Madeleine's love and concern neither begin nor end there. Her world and her concerns embrace people whose basic needs

are not satisfied, those who live on the fringes of society. Before her marriage, Madeleine served as a nurse among the Indians and Eskimos of Alaska. Later, she became active in the League of Women Voters, and in organizing a city-wide store to recycle clothes to needy people. Madeleine's thirst for justice and her capacity to be concerned with people whose needs are not satisfied is an inspiration and incentive to her family as well as others.

VALUES

Personal and societal values have a profound influence on the way we live and the decisions we make. This is true even when those values are unconscious or unarticulated. We tend to value those people, activities, or things that help us fulfill our needs. As an example, suppose John Markham, a senior in high school, has a great need for the respect and esteem of others. He may find sports as a way of meeting that need. Or perhaps dating or studies or a job can provide the respect he needs. As John meets with success—that is, as he feels respected and esteemed by others—he will tend to value the particular activity which led to it more than others. And the stronger his need for respect, the more he will value whatever brings him success.

Jim Robinson knows what his personal values are and consciously incorporates those values into his decisions. Before he was thirty Jim had earned a master's degree in business administration as well as a law degree and had taught at the university level. Even more impressive than his academic accomplishments, however, are the man himself and the values that pervade his life. Robinson has always valued people and their potential. That is why, in his student days, he served as chapter president of the National Affiliation of Concerned Business Students and as vice-president of the

Association of Black Business Students. That is why, in his professional capacity, he worked with the Accounting Aid Society of Metropolitan Detroit to provide free accounting services to over seventy non-profit groups who could not afford to pay for them. And that is why he later became director of New Detroit's Comprehensive Youth Training and Community Involvement Program. Because Robinson values people and their potential, he initiates and works with programs that aim at the positive development of people.

Like Jim Robinson, each of us incorporates a unique blend of talents, needs, and values into our life decisions. To appraise those talents, needs, and values well we must take a positive and penetrating look at ourselves. In a society which measures a person's worth by his or her productive output, it is easy to focus more readily on the negative within ourselves. As we dream a

little, stretch our imagination, project into the future with creative fantasy, we become more life-giving and helpful for ourselves and others. As we point out strengths and talents, we instill confidence and courage. We become more fully human and assist others to do the same.

All our needs and values have to be brought into some sort of balance. We cannot completely ignore needs for respect or love, for instance, in favor of our needs for comfort or safety. On the other hand, we cannot overstress activities which provide us with self-esteem and love while we ignore our physical health.

One way of discovering our needs and values is to write up an analysis of how we spend our time during a given week. If we find that we spend a lot of time practising guitar rather than watching TV or working to earn spending money rather than studying, we will begin to understand what is important to us. These are our values. Discerning our needs is more complicated. Usually, we see needs only when they are way out of balance. If someone is a chronic overeater, for instance, we know that person's eating goes beyond physical needs. And if someone spends much time seeking approval from friends, coaches, and teachers, we might guess that self-esteem is at a low point. Looking back at the four limited perspectives in the last chapter we see that they were based on extremely unbalanced sets of needs.

The Scripture story of the rich young man describes how values reflect needs. He came to Jesus and asked, "What must I do to inherit eternal life?" Since the young man already kept the commandments, Jesus suggested that if he were really serious, he should give away all of his possessions and join Jesus and his disciples. As the story goes, the young man felt he could not do that—"he had many possessions"—and so, sadly, he left Jesus. (Mark 10:17-22).

Several important facts can be drawn from this story. First, we see that this young man's possessions were extremely important to him. Evidently they fulfilled some need of his—security perhaps, or respect and esteem. The young man's needs were excessive, however, to the degree that he could not choose against them—much as he wanted to. He was not free to take the next challenging step toward being fully human, even though he seemed to know Jesus was right. When we value something too strongly, we sometimes reject our own consciences as well as the good advice of others.

This story further illustrates that the challenge to become fully human is not easily taken up. We probably do not know many people who would do what Jesus invited the young man to do. We all probably know quite a few people who would scoff at the idea of giving away hard-earned money. The gesture seems foolish—or heroic—to most of us.

2 The Problem with Heroes

In our life journey toward humanness, we encounter a special problem which the psychologist Maslow labeled "The Jonah Complex." By this he meant that, like Jonah hiding from God, we generally fear our highest possibilities just as much as we do our basest impulses. "We enjoy and even thrill to the godlike possibilities we see in ourselves. . . And yet we simultaneously shiver with weakness, awe, and fear before these very same possibilities." Our fear may tempt us to run away from our best talents rather than develop them. Further, fear may also tempt us to resent the special talents or goodness or beauty in others. It might even lead us to shun heroes or to admire them from afar.

Christianity is a powerful challenge to perfect our talents. It might well frighten off even a good person like the rich young man in the parable just mentioned. So difficult is this vision to live fully, that the writer G. K. Chesterton commented that Christianity had not failed; it simply had never been tried— except once, we might add.

No one is asked to become a Christian hero overnight, however. Like any journey, we make it step by step. It is the direction, set by our fundamental perspective, which is the important consideration. And it is interesting to note that moral heroes do not often think of themselves that way. Their lives are the culmination of hundreds and thousands of small steps—decisions taken one at a time in the right direction. Eventually, as their direction seems more certain to them, they pick up the pace, until finally their lives clearly reflect the compassion of Jesus.

3 Joy and Strength

A recurring challenge in our life journey is to bring talents, needs, and values into some sort of balance. Since talents develop, needs change, and values deepen, this integration is never finished. Further, we run into many conflicts while we are learning to live on our own—especially in our teenage years. And it seems we seldom get our conflicts resolved to our satisfaction because they are too complicated for quick solutions. For instance, in trying to achieve an adult status within our families, we often upset our parents with our conflicting views and plans and our stumbling efforts toward maturity. It sometimes takes many years to reestablish ourselves as family members on a new adult footing. The same is true in coming to terms with our sexuality, discovering our talents, and experiencing mature love and friendship.

We do meet with certain successes along the way, however, which suggest that solving these conflicts by integrating our needs, talents, and values can be a delightful matter. Perhaps we meet someone from the other sex whose friendship affirms our own masculine or feminine self image and who, *at the same time,* is a remarkable advisor and confidant. Maybe we find a job that is challenging and *at the same time* provides some money to free us from having to depend on the family more than we wish. Or perhaps through working with some service group we experience how our ability to help other people *at the same time* helps us to become more caring and compassionate. Perhaps in our disagreements with parents we are able to reach some creative compromises which meet our needs and, *at the same time,* respond to their honest concerns.

Granted that some of our conflicts are extremely difficult to tackle, we find that when we do solve them imaginatively, meeting all sorts of combinations of needs and values at once, the result is a feeling of joy and strength. We feel "more like ourselves." It is this kind of joy and strength that empowers us in our growth.

4 Lifestyles and Careers

The choices of career and lifestyle are major decisions that reflect our fundamental perspective and focus our talents, needs, and values. Lifestyles are ways of *being* in the world; careers are ways of *doing*. Doing is concerned with accomplishments and achievements which can be measured. Being is concerned with living out the truth of our own unique existence. Some people stress being; others stress doing. This is natural. Gradually, as we examine the truth of our own unique existence and enter into its mystery, being and doing become more integral and interdependent—like breathing in and breathing out.

A lifestyle is more encompassing, yet more personal, than a career. It develops from the way we see ourselves, others, the world, and history, and can be narrow or broad, depending on our fundamental perspective. Besides our careers, our lifestyle includes how we decide to occupy our time, what we eat and drink, where we live, how we heat and cool our homes, how and why we travel, the kinds of clothes we wear, and all the little and big things that make up the fabric of daily life. It is our way of being in the world.

A lifestyle is as personal and unique as a world view. It is the way in which we live out our fundamental perspective on the day-to-day level. Even those who have not yet chosen a career already possess a lifestyle, including friendships, entertainment, job, interests, or sports. That lifestyle may reflect certain attitudes: confusion, carefree joy, sexual curiosity, resentments, or combinations of these and other feelings.

A career is a chosen occupation. It is a job, but it should be more than "putting in time." It is a way to earn a living, but it should be more than working to provide life's necessities. As artist or engineer, plumber or writer, community organizer, architect, assembly line worker, energy researcher, or any of a thousand possibilities, our career is what we choose to do with that significant portion of our lives we name "work."

A career choice is important because it is our primary means of doing the works of justice and of shaping history. How we choose our career and live it out stems from how we see ourselves and others in the world. As our fundamental perspective expands, our capacity to make decisions that will have long-range positive impact grows. A wise career decision gives personal satisfaction and fulfillment and makes a significant contribution to society.

A career can be versatile and creative. Tom Templin, for example, had worked for three years toward a degree in fine arts when he decided to try his hand in a business venture with his brother. To his delight he was able to apply principles learned in art to the new task at hand. But business was not Tom's forte. Spurred on by a growing interest in psychology, he returned to the university in his mid-twenties to study psychology. There he met other students with a similar bent. They too were sorting out personal values and setting life directions. Those friendships helped Tom to confirm his own values and to see more clearly how a career in psychology could be personally satisfying and at the same time make a contribution to society. Now a doctoral candidate, Tom is researching behavior patterns and their natural causes. Where this first step in his career will eventually lead is uncertain. But Tom's strong belief in the power of people to shape their lives and surroundings is certain. As a psychologist he hopes to be able to free people from fears that prevent them from tapping that power. How his previous work toward a fine arts degree will fit into all this remains an open question. Perhaps it will be a lifelong hobby, or it may lead to a later second career. Careers, like the journey of life itself, can be full of surprises.

5 Institutions

A career can give us the opportunity to unite with others and thus to extend our influence to more people within a wider time span. We do this through the economic, educational, political, cultural, and religious institutions of society.

Institutions are both products of the past and shapers of the future. They bring decision-making to a social or community level. Ideally, institutions exist to serve the needs of society and not exclusively for their own profit and growth. Institutions can enable us to be more efficient and effective in our goals or they can obstruct and frustrate the accomplishment of our personal goals. When we are motivated and creative, we can channel the energies of almost any institution into the service of humanity.

Walter Haas has established a reputation as a progressive, far-sighted, socially responsible leader in business. A top executive of the Levi Strauss & Company, Haas believes that personal decisions brought to a social or community level serve the needs of society far beyond what one individual can do. Haas's personal stance and philosophy have permeated many levels of the company and contributed significantly to its corporate thrust. Consequently, the San Francisco-based jeans company has been cited numerous times for its social sensitivities. It is an acknowledged leader in product quality, minority employment (including officials and managers), and innovative support of community-oriented projects.

These community-oriented projects range from ecology to education. At more than thirty Levi Strauss facilities, community relations teams have been formed and funded with seed money to support employees engaged in local projects in the public interest. This encourages employees to use corporation resources creatively to deal with social problems. The

Sister Clarita Trujillo
Missionary Sister

Wonderful things happen when Clarita Trujillo puts her hand to the task. They happen not so much because *she does* the task, but because she gets others to do it! Clarita is a "people-prodder" who for almost twenty years has promoted the social, political, and spiritual well-being of people in California, Texas, Colorado, and her native New Mexico.

"We live in an exciting era . . . a great awakening in the consciousness of people . . . a time of change . . ." Dark eyes shining, Clarita elaborates on how we can flavor that change with love and Christian freedom. The key, she believes, lies in helping people to recognize needs and to actualize their talents to meet those needs.

At the invitation of Archbishop Sanchez, Sister Clarita assessed the needs and strengths of twelve parishes in northeastern New Mexico. Needs were basic: better housing, quality education, and economic development. Specifically, people needed the urban-oriented Church to become more effectively present in their rural and semi-rural communities. Clarita's recommendations were specific too: develop a pastoral program, redistribute human and financial resources, appoint a Director of Development to lobby for economic development and social needs.

Clarita's background, education, and experience are well suited to her work as a "people-prodder." She grew up with four brothers in El Rito, a small village in the mountains of New Mexico. Job opportunities were scarce when she graduated from high school, so Clarita went to Denver and worked for an insurance company. Five years later she joined the Victory Noll Missionary Sisters in Huntington, Indiana, and a wide range of possibilities opened to her.

Clarita has taught religion; visited in hospitals, nursing homes, and jails; and worked in various neighborhood and community projects. One of 300 Victory Noll Missionary Sisters whose hopes and dreams she shares, Clarita gives and receives the encouragement and challenge necessary to sustain hope as she works toward justice.

company does not take a corporate stand on political issues, but it encourages workers to make personal political decisions and to act on them. For example, following the United States invasion of Cambodia in the late sixties, the company urged employees to write or to wire their views—on company time and at company expense—to the President and to Congress.

Walter Haas is not alone in his belief that decisions brought to a social or community level can have a profound impact on society. Individual decision makers in institutions can be unwise and inhumane profiteers, or they can be wise and sensitive imagineers who mobilize an institution's power to serve the needs of society.

We too can choose careers in the economic, educational, political, cultural, or religious institutions of society and so channel the energies of these institutions for the service of humanity.

6 Moving Beyond Ourselves

Our personal decisions affect others directly.

When Mary DeBruce, a high school student, decided to care for the children of a neighbor whose wife was in the hospital, her decision lessened the weight of that neighbor's already heavy burden. When she decided to write to her senator urging him to vote in favor of a particular food bill that was being debated in Congress, she joined thousands of others to support a law that now makes life a little less difficult for poor people. On another occasion when Mary decided to boycott a certain company's products because she believed that company guilty of unjust marketing practices, she joined with many others in registering disapproval of those practices and in urging their dis-

**continuance. Like Mary, each of us can make decisions
that positively affect other people.**

Other people's decisions affect us directly. A friend's decision to
move to a different location can make us realize how much we
cherish that friend. An administrator's decision to raise tuition or
a legislature's decision to raise taxes can set us scrambling to
readjust an already strained budget. The seemingly far-removed
decisions of scientists to produce nuclear power, of medical researchers to develop a polio or smallpox vaccine, and of a weary
black woman to keep her seat on a Montgomery bus have affected
our lives more profoundly than most of us realize.

Personal decisions often have greater impact than we realize.

In 1938, a young Spaniard traveled to Japan where he worked as medic, teacher, and counselor for more than a quarter of a century. August 6, 1945, forever divides those years. He was in Hiroshima. At 8:15 in the morning a single American plane flew over the city and dropped the bomb that killed nearly 80,000 people and injured at least that many more. The Spaniard survived and used his medical skill and compassion to minister to the tragically burned and frightened victims. That Spaniard's name is Pedro Arrupe. Later, as religious leader of the worldwide Society of Jesus, he became known throughout the world as a man of hope.

Arrupe had nothing to do with the decision to bomb Hiroshima, but he felt its impact profoundly. For him, the events of that August morning image a frightened and disfigured world. Arrupe's legacy of hope urges all of us to examine the roots of infection that cause such havoc and to tend the wounds of our world according to our talents and opportunities.

Ultimately, those roots of infection are found within our own hearts. To look inward—to study our personal history—is not to deny the injustice structured into the very fabric of our institutions. Nor is it to deny the need to bring personal decisions to a social or community level. Rather, it is to acknowledge that behind every structure and within every institution a personal or collective will is responsible. Our decisions create just or unjust structures; our decisions can change those structures. When we are ill-informed, shortsighted, or selfish, our fundamental perspective is narrow and our decisions can perpetuate injustice. When we are well-informed and concerned for those beyond our immediate time and space framework, our decisions can imagineer a future that is just and worthy to be called human.

Effective decisions do not just "happen." We make conscious

choices in the midst of ambiguity. Ordinarily we go through a simple but sometimes difficult process to arrive at an effective decision. With necessarily limited vision we journey through life, making decisions on the basis of whatever pertinent information is available. As we become more conscious of ourselves as decision makers, we become more conscious of these basic facts:

1) **We have the potential to shape our environment by our personal decisions.**

2) **We are responsible for the decisions we make or fail to make.**

3) **When needs are excessive or out of balance, it is difficult to make wise decisions.**

4) **We can make wise and effective career and life-style decisions as we come to understand more deeply our talents, needs, and values.**

REVIEW QUESTIONS

1) **How did George Bernard Shaw's fundamental perspective affect his life journey?**

2) **What lesson can be learned from the parable of the talents? What three things does the story of the talents reveal about each of us?**

3) **What are the general categories of needs, according to the psychologist Abraham H. Maslow? How are these categories related?**

4) **How does the Scripture story of the rich young man describe the effect of personal needs on one's values?**

5) **What is meant by the "Jonah complex"?**

6) **What types of conflicts are often created as we try to achieve an adult status within our families?**

7) What is the difference between a lifestyle and a career? Why are they important?

8) What role can institutions play in shaping the future?

9) Why is it so important that we study our "personal history" as we try to create a more livable and more lovable world?

3
Lifestyle and Career Choices:
Approaches to Decision-Making

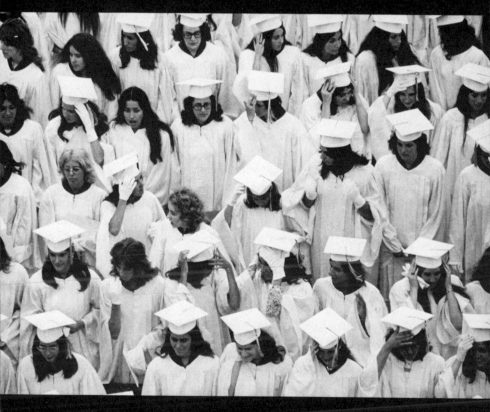

To live is to change
and to be perfect
is to have changed often.
John Cardinal Newman

Decision-making means choosing one particular course of action from among a number of alternatives. Action can follow a decision, but decision must precede action. Small decisions of every day often go unnoticed until we reflect on them in the broader context of life. Major decisions, on the other hand, demand conscious reflection. Major decisions can lead to significant change and often grow out of a process which can be plagued with doubt and ambiguity.

Choosing a career or a particular style of life are major decisions that demand conscious reflection. If we do not consciously choose a career or lifestyle, we might drift through life at the mercy of circumstances. Only rarely do we choose a career or make lifestyle decisions with ease and clarity. More often we move tentatively in a particular direction, developing personal talents, recognizing personal needs, and deepening personal values. This brings some degree of clarity which either strengthens the decision we seem to be moving toward or shows it to be lacking in some way. Through a process of testing, developing and using our talents, evaluating, and testing again, we are able to make decisions which point the way to effective action.

Some young people find it difficult to be patient with this dynamic but often gradual process of discovery. Youth is a time when we struggle to adopt our own attitudes and to do our own thinking. It is a time when we seek to discover our talents, to make our own decisions, and to find what "fits" with our personality. This is often done gropingly, and sometimes in anguish.

The struggle to be a whole, mature, integrated person, a fully human, just and loving person is never finished. We can always be better. Every decision we make can bring us closer to reaching our full human potential for doing the works of justice.

The approaches to decision-making we examine here complement each other. The first approach is based on rational judgment. It recognizes that we make decisions based upon our understanding of ourselves—talents, needs, and values—as well as the external circumstances of our lives. The second approach—prayerful discernment—brings all these considerations into the realm of faith. By incorporating prayer and religious experience into the fabric of decision-making, prayerful discernment puts us in touch with a deeper knowledge of our total selves and with the Christian perspective. These two approaches are not mutually exclusive, since our faith builds on rather than substitutes for rational judgment.

1 Rational Judgment

Most people think seriously when they are faced with a major decision. The process looks deceivingly simple on paper:

1) *Gather* a reasonable amount of information.
2) *Interpret* that information thoroughly and objectively.
3) *Choose* one course of action from among the alternatives.
4) *Implement* the decision by appropriate action.
5) *Evaluate* the decision in view of its effects.

A CASE STUDY

Greg Roman used this approach to make a major career decision. All through high school his primary interest was playing his guitar. With little study and little thought of his future, Greg breezed through school and graduated with surprisingly high grades. Then, for several years he drifted from one part-time job to another. When he entered the university Greg faced his first

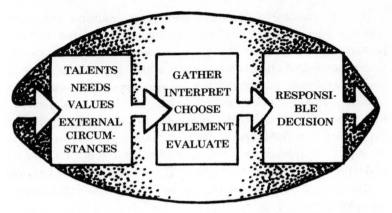

MAKING DECISIONS WITH RATIONAL JUDGMENT. This figure shows how talents, needs, and values feed into the five steps of decision-making that lead to a responsible decision.

real challenge. There he discovered talents he never knew he had—and never before cared about.

In his senior year, Greg excelled in English and was majoring in journalism. A hard-working reporter for the university's daily paper, he was favored for a spot on one of the city's papers after graduation. But Greg's interest in music continued. His four summers as camp counselor had shown him that music can be an effective means to break down the barriers of prejudice and to build up trust among people. Journalism can be that too, he knew, and he had the talent to do it well. The question nagged: "Which is the better career route for me—music or journalism?"

Here are some questions that Greg considered as he gathered and interpreted pertinent information: What are my realistic opportunities in journalism? In music? How could journalism tap my talents? Fill my needs? Reflect my values? How could music do these things? What impact would a career in journalism or in music contribute to the wider society? Greg talked with people in both fields to find out what they were actually doing and how satisfied they were in their work.

When he was convinced that he had gathered enough information and interpreted it as best he could, Greg lined up his options.

He asked himself "What would happen if . . ." and began to imagine several alternatives. It was not so simple as "music or journalism" but, until the alternatives were clear, the possibility of a wise choice was limited. After some months of indecision, Greg decided to pursue a career in journalism. Action followed choice and evaluation followed action. As he lives out his decision, Greg continues to evaluate its effects and to judge its consequences for himself and others.

1) Greg's use of the five steps illustrates sound judgment at work in making a major decision. A sound decision is rooted in reality. It is built on facts. The first step toward making a sound decision is to gather enough pertinent information. We need to learn as much as possible about the circumstances surrounding the decision. If we think we might like to pursue a career in business, medicine, art, or any other field, it is essential that we understand both the opportunities and the difficulties that such a career would probably involve. We can do this by talking with people already working in that field, by reading and discussing with a friend or counselor.

Gradually, as we collect information we are able to move from a broad general understanding to a more specific grasp of what that career might entail. The word *might* is important here. Gathering information can never give a precise picture of what a career could eventually become, since a career is so individually personal. Some people stagnate in what seems an exciting and challenging career; others discover ways to be fully human even in careers that seem ordinary and mundane. The reason for this is closely linked to how differently people see their personal talents, needs, and values. Understood and appreciated, these talents, needs, and values are valuable personal building blocks for gathering the information that is essential for sound decisions. Unrecognized and unappreciated, they make information gathering necessarily incomplete and sound decisions highly unlikely.

2) After we have gathered a reasonable amount of information

we move to the task of interpreting that information as thoroughly and objectively as possible. It is not easy to be thorough; it is even more difficult to be objective. Our culture's values and our own unconscious needs and values can thwart a complete and honest interpretation of facts. As in the first step, a friend, parent, or counselor can be very helpful as we try to assess and understand the facts we have gathered.

3) Choosing one course of action from among a number of alternatives is the core of decision-making. It includes asking "What would happen if . . . ?" and letting our imaginations play with options. It includes weighing advantages and disadvantages of several possible choices. This step is an opportunity to "try on" different roles, careers, and lifestyles to see how they fit with what is most authentically "me." It can be fun because it is creative and innovative; it can be difficult because to *choose* necessarily closes some doors and opens others. We discover that choosing is freedom as well as responsibility.

4) To implement a major decision may require time, energy, stamina, and it may create some frustration. It often requires meeting short-term goals that make the long-term ones possible. Anyone who wants to become effective in a career must be willing to work hard and to make the many decisions along the way that support the eventual goal. If I decide to be an agricultural technician in a developing country, for example, I have to study the language and culture of the people in addition to acquiring the necessary technical knowledge and skill. If I want to do a good job in community organizing, I must develop political expertise plus the ability to listen to people and their needs. If I want to live in a way that respects nature and looks to the welfare of future generations, I have to make many daily decisions which support that lifestyle. To implement a major decision is no easy task.

5) As the consequences of a major decision begin to unfold, we can evaluate that decision in view of its effects. Either we can be

strengthened in knowing it is a good decision, or we can find that it does not really fit with our particular blend of talents, needs, and values, and the external circumstances of our lives. Judging the consequences of a decision is crucial to sound decision-making. In addition to requiring time and energy, major decisions often require the willingness to live in ambiguity while we test the decision.

This testing process gives additional information which in turn affirms or raises questions about the decision. When questions predominate, the process can begin again. In the end, we make a decision to go in a particular direction, and we affirm our decision by our actions.

2 Prayerful Discernment

People who possess a vital religious faith express and incorporate that faith into the process of decision-making. They let faith and a thirst for justice provoke, inform, and shape their decisions. That is the essence of prayerful discernment.

Prayerful discernment is a way of living and making decisions that is rooted in faith, in an experience of God. It is in no way a substitute for rational judgment. Rather, it expands upon rational judgment and enables us to examine issues at a deeper level—within our personal relationship with God. Through prayerful discernment we deepen that relationship. Like the psalmist long ago we ask, "Yahweh, make your ways known to me, teach me your paths. Set me in the way of your truth, and teach me, for you are the God who saves me" (Psalm 25:4-5).

PRAYER

Our innate religious sense awakens in us a longing for God. That longing is the beginning of the dialogue with God that we call prayer. Prayer is listening for God. Since God can speak to us in a wide variety of ways, prayer can take a wide variety of forms.

God can speak through a friend, through feelings of discontent or of joy, through silence, through events we ourselves plan, or through circumstances that catch us by surprise. God's ways are as countless as the stars and they are specially designed for each person. Fortunately for us, God does not limit dialogue to our times of formal prayer. And always, God communicates love. To make a major decision, the choice of a career or a style of life, without listening for that word of love is like not listening to the advice of a good friend.

Prayer is a way of reaching out and at the same time reaching into our deepest selves. In listening for God beyond, surprisingly we hear within ourselves a lot about our deep needs and hurts, and we find wisdom at our core. When we open up to others at any time, in love or in compassion, we open ourselves to God. It can happen because a sunrise strikes awe in us. It can happen when we are concentrating on sports or on studies. It can happen when we help younger brothers or sisters. This is prayer.

Prayer frees us from compulsion by providing us with an open, loving stance for decision-making. Most of us are amateur and unsophisticated in the process of listening for God. God often speaks so softly that he is drowned out by our shoutings, our loud music, and our flurry of activities. Think back to the limited perspectives described in chapter 1. In each of those cases, the stress caused by insecurity, powerlessness, and frustration produced a narrow or distorted perspective.

Too often we do not hear God's word of love until we are stopped in our tracks by an accident, sickness, or even a death. These cause us to think and to pray. Sometimes it is rather late, and we have already undertaken commitments that cannot responsibly be turned from. For a person of faith to make free, well-founded, and long-lasting decisions about career or lifestyle, it is essential to pray and to discern at our core the word of God.

How often do we let "Jonah's" fear of excellence force us to quit trying or not attempt something? How often do we choose the "sure thing" rather than risk trying for a better job, a deeper friendship, a chance at college or a scholarship? When we let prayer flow through our decisions, that is, when we listen for God, we silence for the moment that sort of banal chat we sometimes carry on within ourselves about how we cannot do this or that.

DISCERNMENT

Prayer and discernment go hand in hand. Discernment is a set of sensitive skills that enable us to better listen for God's word of love. It is based on these experiences of men and women:

1) God speaks to us through the persons, places, events, and circumstances of our daily lives.

2) God calls us to certain decisions, paths, and life goals. From the several alternatives of morally good decisions and actions that we might choose, one of them is the best response to the call of God here and now.

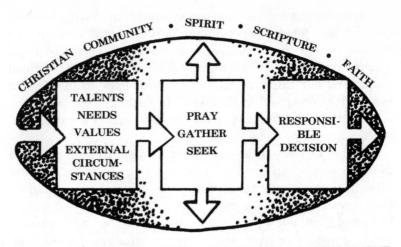

MAKING DECISIONS WITH PRAYERFUL DISCERNMENT.
This figure illustrates how talents, needs, and values feed into the three
stages of prayerful discernment that lead to a responsible decision.

3) God will reveal his preference and choice for us if we ask and make an effort to listen.

Decisions aided by prayerful discernment can provide a shortcut through the often agonizing process of decision-making. The words of Jesus in the New Testament contain wisdom that most of us could achieve only after decades of difficult experience. In the same way, discernment aids us in reaching decisions that probably would be much more difficult, take much longer, and whose results would not be as satisfying without our listening for God.

The question now becomes, "How do I best hear, perceive, and discern what God is saying?" Discernment is a delicate process. First, we need an attitude of openness and attentiveness to God. Sometimes God's message is clear. Much more often, especially in complex situations, it is necessary to listen sensitively and to develop some mechanism for interpreting what may seem to be varying messages. This process is not quick, easy, or totally unambiguous.

There are three stages in the discernment process:

1) *Praying for God's light and guidance.* This involves asking for God's help and being open and attentive to the profound feelings we experience as we reflect upon our decision.

2) *Gathering all available evidence for judgment.* This includes paying attention to the concrete circumstances (talents, needs, values, aspirations), the demands of a particular career and lifestyle, and how well a career or lifestyle meets our perspective as Christians. For example, does this decision reflect hope and imagination? By it, are we better able to treat other people in caring, compassionate ways? This step also includes dialogue with people who have special competency.

3) *Seeking confirmation* during every stage of the discernment process. Confirmation most often takes the form of interior tranquility, that is, of quiet, gentle peace. This peace is at our deepest level. It does not eliminate all anxieties or fears, but is an awareness of peace at the core of our being. It is a taste of God's peace and joy.

Asking for God's guidance, gathering all available evidence, and continually seeking confirmation are not really three successive steps to be adhered to in strict order. Rather, by continually intermingling all of them, we move toward the ultimate decision. Even after a "final" judgment is reached (for example, to learn agricultural economics in order to help feed the hungry, or to live a life of voluntary simplicity), that decision is still open to verification through new experiences. Indeed, further discernment *should* take place on the basis of experiences coming from taking new action.

THE SPIRITUAL EXERCISES

Many people find the *Spiritual Exercises of St. Ignatius of Loyola* a great help in the process of discerning God's will for them. The *Spiritual Exercises* can be a personal and profound experience of God. Often they mark the beginning of a deep interior peace that helps us to make future decisions with vision and clarity. A word of warning is in order here: the *Exercises* are not intended to be read as a book, but to be prayed through with someone experienced as a director, ordinarily in some days of quiet.

The *Spiritual Exercises* provide several concrete aids to discernment. The first of these is that we should visualize a young person much like ourselves in age, background, talents, interests, and values.

We should imagine that person coming to us and asking us for help and advice in making a career or lifestyle decision. How would we help that young man or woman to outline the alternatives and sort through the evidence? What help and advice would we give? That same advice we might well apply to ourselves.

A second technique to aid discernment is this:

We should visualize ourselves at the moment of death, looking back over our lives. From that perspective, what choice or decision would we want to have made earlier in life? What would we like to have done with our life? The answer to those questions could well be an important element in our decision-making.

A third technique can be especially helpful:

We should visualize ourselves before God after death. From the vantage point of God's love, what career choice or way of life would we have wanted to follow?

This too could provide helpful data for making a career or lifestyle decision.

The purpose of these three techniques is to situate decision-making in the Christian perspective and at the same time in a profoundly personal one. Each technique helps us to get beyond the immediate here and now, and to look at major decisions in a broader time and space framework. Each technique also puts us in touch with our deepest personal aspirations and values. They can be of great value as we strive to make wise, effective, and satisfying decisions. Then, with a thirst for justice as our driving force, our decisions and actions can further God's love in human history.

Prayerful discernment can help us to arrive at freer decisions. When we are blinded by our limited experiences, biases, loves and hates, our perception of reality becomes blurred and discernment becomes very difficult. When we are preoccupied with the need for food and security, our vision becomes so narrow that discernment is almost impossible. Prayerful discernment enables us to overcome our blindness and distorted perception. It enables us to hear more deeply the word and the will of God in our lives. Prayer is frequent in a discerning person's life.

3 Living Out Our Decisions

There is no way to predict with absolute certainty that our career and lifestyle decisions will work out the way we hope and dream that they will. Even important decisions, once carefully and conscientiously made, can lose their vitality and driving force as time passes and circumstances change. Perhaps this uncertainty is due to age, experience, growth in wisdom or retreat into selfishness, but the evidence is clear and abundant. The choice of a marriage partner, for example, is one of the most important decisions a person can make. Yet, lately, partners in one out of every three marriages in the United States make their way to divorce courts to change their decisions.

René Dubos
Microbiologist and Ecologist

René Dubos' life is an intriguing blend. As a microbiologist he studies the most minute forms of life; as an ecologist he studies the interplay between all living things and the environment. For Dubos these are not two worlds, but one.

Research for his doctorate at Rutgers University set Dubos on a course that was to bring these two worlds together. His experiments showed that, under certain conditions, microorganisms could actually decompose the cell walls of plants. This insight heightened his awareness of the profound influence that environment has on biological processes and helped to shape decisions affecting subsequent phases of his career. The effects that environmental and social forces exert on human life became the subject of his long and illustrious career in research, writing, and teaching.

Dubos first demonstrated the possibility of obtaining antibacterial drugs from the microorganisms found in soil. This pioneering discovery paved the way for others to develop penicillin and other antibiotics for medical use.

Except for two years at Harvard, Dubos has done all his research and teaching at Rockefeller Institute in New York City. He has written numerous books and publications including *So Human an Animal* which received a Pulitzer Prize in 1969. In preparation for the United Nations Conference on the Human Environment, Dubos, together with Barbara Ward, co-authored *Only One Earth*. A sentence in its introduction catches the meaning and spirit of Dubos' career. It might well be his legacy and challenge to today's decision makers: "Man not only survives and functions in his environment, he shapes it and he is shaped by it."

There are ways, however, to assure that the strength and vitality of solid, well-founded decisions will continue throughout our life journey. Two approaches for making major decisions have already been examined. Now two approaches for continuing to live out those decisions will be examined.

The first approach is based on rational judgment and is called critical reflection. The second allows faith and prayer to penetrate rational judgment. It is called prayerful assessment. From their different perspectives, these approaches can help us to understand where we have been, where we are now, and in what direction we are headed. They can further help us to understand the motives beneath our decisions and actions. Neither critical reflection nor prayerful assessment rule out changes or new directions. Rather, they assure that changes or new directions will be thoughtful and well-founded and not unduly influenced by short-term emotions.

CRITICAL REFLECTION

Critical reflection is a way to examine our daily decisions, actions, and motivations in light of personal long-term goals and major decisions. When we reflect critically on our lives, we can see ourselves in relationship to other persons and can evaluate how our decisions and actions promote or prevent the possibility of full human life. In addition, we can gain deeper insight into our talents, needs, and values and their motivational power. The process of critical reflection is both simple and profound:

1) *recollect* and center myself.
2) *survey my decisions and actions* over a particular period of time.
3) *search out the underlying motivation* of those decisions and actions.
4) *evaluate effects.*
5) *renew or change my course of action.*

Greg Roman's experience illustrates how critical reflection influences his life journey. After some months of indecision, Greg decided to pursue a career in journalism. His experience as a reporter for his school paper prepared him for work on the staff of a city newspaper. Greg graduated, moved from his parents' home to a small apartment close to work, and began life on his own.

1) Each night Greg takes a few minutes to review his day. Playing his guitar helps him to relax and unwind after the day's hectic pace. This is his time for centering and recollecting himself. Relaxed, he sits quietly and allows the day's events to flow through his consciousness. There were many feelings: satisfaction, happiness, anxiety, anger, excitement, confusion. There were many activities too: at work, at home, with friends. Some feelings were so fleeting and some activities so absorbing that he must take time to center himself and become conscious of them before he is ready to move on to the next phase of critical reflection.

2) Greg surveys his day's decisions and actions by examining how they fit with his personal long-term goals and major decisions. Having already decided on a career in journalism, he examines his use of time and talents to determine whether he contributed his best efforts in the newsroom. Being realistic, Greg knows that every activity has some routine or unattractive aspects. Even in those situations, he can realize the goals he has set for himself.

There are other aspects of his day too—having lunch with co-workers, buying necessities for his apartment, being a "big brother" to a fatherless boy, and socializing with friends. Greg surveys his decisions and actions in these situations, noting how they fit with his decision to live a relatively simple lifestyle. He reflects on the quality of his relationships with friends and co-workers and on his personal sense of well-being.

3) Surveying his daily decisions and actions provides Greg

with valuable insight into his personal motivation. He sees that sometimes his need for esteem is an overriding factor, and that at other times his need for security dominates. Greg is happiest when he recognizes that his small daily decisions support his personal long-term goals and major decisions. Perhaps even more important, he can sense harmony or conflict between his career and lifestyle.

4) Having searched out the underlying motivations for his decisions and actions, Greg proceeds to evaluate their effects. He examines how his decisions interact with those of other people to determine the quality of his immediate environment and how they fit with his expanding perspective. He thus judges the impact of his personal decisions on the wider society.

5) Finally, Greg renews his earlier decision to be a positive force in journalism and in every aspect of his life. His short time of critical reflection strengthens him with new insight and purpose. Continuing in this daily practice can strengthen his career and lifestyle decisions and gradually make them more mutually supportive. It may prepare him for changes and new directions as a result of new self-knowledge. It will certainly help him to become more mature, more fully human, and a more positive force for justice in society.

PRAYERFUL ASSESSMENT

Prayerful assessment is a second approach to examine our daily decisions, actions, and motivations. When we choose this approach, we allow faith and an experience of God to affect our critical reflection so we see our lives at a deeper level. Speaking to God and, more importantly, listening for God, helps us to recognize love in all the events of our life journey. It prepares for and leads into the honest evaluation known as prayerful assessment.

The five phases of prayerful assessment correspond roughly to the five steps of critical reflection:

1) recollect and center myself, *asking for God's help and insight.*

2) *thank God* for gifts.

3) survey my decisions and actions over a particular period of time, *asking God to show me his way* of seeing those decisions and actions.

4) evaluate effects, *talking these over with God.*

5) renew or change my course of action, *affirming my decision* to follow God's call in my life.

Ann Reardon illustrates the use of prayerful assessment. As a high school senior she enjoyed reading Scripture and developed a habit of daily prayer. God became personal for her, and prayer a way of communicating with God, much like friends communicate with one another. Ann's habit of prayer deepened her awareness of God's action in her life. Now as a college sophomore, Ann is not yet sure of her career direction, but she has already chosen a simple lifestyle.

Ann frequently begins her talk with God by reading a favorite poem or a psalm. This is her way to recollect and to center herself, to be in tune with God. She asks for God's help so that she can be sensitive to God's presence in their conversation. This is centering. It is the essential first phase of prayerful assessment.

Thanking God, the second phase, flows naturally. Ann's faith and habit of prayer help her to see God in the specific people and events of her day. As she lets the images of those people and events fill her consciousness, she recognizes them as gifts and thanks God for them.

Next, Ann surveys her day's decisions and actions by talking them over with God, much as we might talk over our day with a close friend. She asks to see the day as God sees it, that is, to see how God is present. She reviews her decisions and actions from several different angles: as student, part-time office worker, volunteer worker at a neighborhood center, and family member. She further reviews how the day's small decisions and actions fit with her long-term decision to live as a Christian in caring, generous

Beverly Steigerwald
Wife, Mother, and Artist

Beverly Steigerwald describes her life in one word: "hectic." But "hectic" only skims the surface of the life of this woman whose primary career is marriage and being mother to seven growing children. Beneath that surface is the deeply sensitive spirit of an artist.

To Bev, being wife and mother has meant to rejoice anew in the wonders of life—to share discovery and thus to rediscover. It has also meant hours of routine work at home, of waiting in dentists' offices, and of driving children to and from various activities. This was Bev's thinking time, time to reflect on what she had recently experienced, and to see the visual image of the situation. Then, when the youngest child went off to school and the work load changed intensity, the images were there, not yet fully developed, but ready at hand. With clay and wax and new-found time, Bev turned to sculpturing.

"Impressively conceived observations of man in his relationship to his gods and to each other" is the way Bev describes her subject matter. Her decision to express in bronze some of humankind's most deeply felt realities grew out of sensitivity and experience. A frustrating time on jury duty led to "Justice without Truth." "A New World A'Coming" was created in the midst of civil rights struggles, and "A Nation at War" in sorrow over the war in Ireland. "Morning Song" captures the sheer ecstacy of life, while "The Way of the Pilgrim" witnesses to life's transitory nature.

To see these works of art is somehow to be in touch with the human spirit they so beautifully capture. Bev's work is the fruit of active contemplation. It feeds on an active life. As wife, mother, and artist she blends career and lifestyle into one vibrant whole.

ways. In this time of honest assessment, Ann gains insight into God's action in her life and into her response. As she gets to know herself, her friendship with God deepens.

Ann moves easily from surveying her decisions and actions to evaluating their effects. Ann knows the effects reach far beyond what she can see or judge. Nevertheless, there are some effects that she *can* judge. She considers how her decisions and actions fit with her Christian perspective and how they impinge on family, friends, and the wider society.

Finally, Ann proceeds to the final phase of prayerful assessment by affirming her intention to live in simplicity and to follow God's call in her life. Looking ahead to the immediate future, she asks for a deeper sensitivity to the people and events that will be part of that future.

Prayerful assessment strengthens Ann to live out her major decisions with vision and enthusiasm as she comes to see them in an ever broadening Christian perspective.

FINDING A DIRECTION

Critical reflection and prayerful assessment are personal activities. Both have a built-in natural progression and broad general direction, but no one uses them in precisely the same way. The frequency with which we examine our lives and the process we use can be adapted to suit personal needs.

Some people examine their lives every day; others do so several times each week. Still others take a more leisurely look at their lives once each week or once each month. Experience can help us to discover the time, place, and frequency best suited to our individual needs.

Whatever its frequency, the process of critical reflection and prayerful assessment remains basically the same. Whatever importance we give to any one particular step or phase, each step is integral to the process. Again, experience can help us to discover our personal style.

Faithful and conscientious use of critical reflection and prayerful assessment will give vitality and a sense of direction to our life journey. Then, as time passes and circumstances change, we too will change, growing in our capacity to cherish life's mystery and to realize its potential.

REVIEW QUESTIONS

1) What is decision-making?

2) What are two ways that we might approach our major decisions? How do they differ and complement each other?

3) What important steps should we take when we face a major decision? Why is this process sometimes difficult?

4) What is prayer? How does our innate religious sense prepare us for prayer?

5) What is discernment? What is the basis for this mode of decision-making? What are its three stages?

6) How does prayerful discernment affect our decisions?

7) What three techniques are suggested by the *Spiritual Exercises* as concrete aids to discernment?

8) How does critical reflection help us to evaluate our decisions and keep a direction in our lives?

9) How can prayerful assessment help us to enter more deeply into the mystery of our life journey?

When our days become dreary
with low-hovering clouds
and our nights become darker
than a thousand midnights,
we will know that we are living

in a creative turmoil
of a genuine civilization
struggling to be born.

Martin Luther King, Jr.

79

1 Our Cultural Values

When we consider the number of conflicting messages which we receive from our culture each day, we can readily see the benefits of developing our sense of judgment and our capacity for prayer in decision-making. Although we must be individually responsible for our decisions, we do not choose our perspectives or our values or make our decisions in strict privacy. On the contrary, we are confronted daily with thousands of messages telling us what is important.

For example, our parents want us to be successful and moral. Our friends want us to be fun, available—"with it." Our teachers and coaches want us to be alert and quick-witted.

Beyond these helpful people, we are drenched with TV ads selling us ways to "come alive" in our culture by ridding ourselves of yellow teeth, bad breath, underarm odor, pimples, dark hair, leg hair, headaches, and tension. Instead, according to the commercials, we should attach to ourselves false eyelashes, false fingernails, moist smiles, new jeans, new cars, beer bottles, wine glasses, ample young women or dashing young men, briefcases, tickets to warm, sunny places and all kinds of unnecessary food.

At the same time, the radio is playing hundreds of songs between its commercials, suggesting all sorts of anti-cultural or rebellious activities—everything from losing oneself in drugs to finding oneself in the stars.

Along with the many values which we are exposed to in our relationships and in various communications media, unknowingly we have acquired some subtle, but very influential values from our culture itself. In North America, mobility is a prime example.

For us, the transition from childhood to adulthood is symbolized by the driver's license. It was not always this way. After World War II, the super highways were begun as a deterrent to nuclear war. They promised quick evacuation of cities in case of a Russian attack. Suburbs grew along the easy access routes, the road system expanded to link cities, and the automobile became a way of life. This situation affects many of us as individuals.

It is not wrong to value mobility. Mobility, like most things, is good or bad depending upon how we deal with it and why we value it. When mobility becomes too important, it becomes a part of our identity or identified with our survival needs, and we become frightened by anything that might threaten it. Recent gasoline shortages, for example, have caused anxiety for many of us. As a result, we are less able to deal imaginatively and justly with any crises or decisions regarding mobility. When we blindly accept cultural values like mobility, it becomes difficult to determine what our personal values are.

Each of the following cases reveals a value or values that we may have adopted unknowingly as a result of growing up in North American culture. Sometimes we may be aware of these cultural values; at other times we may not give them much thought. Nevertheless, they can affect, subtly but powerfully, the way we live from day to day and even our major lifestyle and career decisions.

THE FIRST SHOT

Chuck awoke in a tense mood on the morning of his twelfth birthday. His father was taking him hunting. This was the first time he would shoot a gun. Chuck did not particularly look forward to spending a day in the forest with his father, looking for animals. Chuck's father was a superb marksman, and to him the ability to shoot was a sign of virility. Chuck's father often told him how *he* had accompanied *his* father to the woods for his first hunting trip on his twelfth birthday. In fact, this ritual had been going on for a couple of generations.

Later in the day, after Chuck's father showed him how to load and fire his gun, both man and boy started watching for beavers. Chuck thought back to his days in school. There were several pets in the laboratory that were his to care for and to raise. He had a fascination for small animals.

Suddenly Chuck's father spotted a beaver nursing her small ones. He whispered to Chuck to take aim and fire. Chuck fired. The animal fell dead. The young ones scurried away in fright. Chuck felt sick but his father gave him an approving slap on the back.

What values are in conflict here? Which would you term cultural values? Do you agree or disagree with them in this case? Why?

IN DEFENSE OF HOME

When Leah was twenty, she left her hometown, Shaker Heights, to join a kibbutz in Israel. She liked her new way of life so much that she became an Israeli citizen. Last month she returned to Shaker Heights to visit her family. She discovered that her two older married sisters had been spending long hours in the state legislature working against passage of the Equal Rights Amendment. "When a country forces a woman to take up arms," they said, "it has lost its respect for women."

Leah shocked her family by telling them that not only had she been drafted but she had fought in skirmishes with enemy guerillas to defend her kibbutz.

What values are in conflict here? Which would you term cultural values? Do you agree or disagree with them in this case? Why?

YOU BE THE WHITE PARENT

Your twenty-one-year-old daughter has been dating a black man just graduated from college. She announces that they have decided to get married. Both are mature young people and seem capable of handling marital responsibilities. What advice will you give her?

What values might be in conflict here? Which would you term cultural values? Do you agree or disagree with them? Why?

COOKING IS HIS CRAFT

Ms. Cunneen is principal of Kenwood's suburban high school. There is an opening in the home economics department for a teacher in cooking and nutrition. Several women have applied, but the most qualified applicant is Gregory Canlis, a thirty-three-year-old, single, Lebanese-American. For several years Mr. Canlis worked in his father's restaurant business where he learned valuable lessons in the art of gourmet cooking. Then he went to graduate school to major in education. He has excellent references both from his department and from the school where he did his practice teaching.

Ms. Cunneen knows, however, that if she hires Mr. Canlis, many parents and some students will be upset. The school has traditionally sought married women for the job since it tries to teach girls not only how to cook but how to act in a family situation.

What values are in conflict here? Which ones would you term cultural values? Do you agree or disagree with them in this case? Why?

CINDERELLA SINGS THE BLUES

When Sam and Jane Willowby came home from school, they noted a large sign on the laundry door. "Washwoman quits. Take care of your own clothes." Their mother, Mary, explained her action. It was now time for each one in the family to take responsibility for his or her own laundry. She would no longer be a "domestic slave."

Sam was angry. He had a football scholarship at school. Between the time he needed for sports and schoolwork, he would have no time to wash and iron his own clothes. "Don't look at me," his sister said. "Just because I'm a girl I'm not going to play Cinderella for the family. I have important things to do too."

Mr. Willowby, a sales representative, tried to change his wife's mind. He argued that he needed all the extra time he has at home

to devise new sales strategies. But Mrs. Willowby is determined: "No one person in a family should have to do all the dull, repetitious tasks."

What values are in conflict here? Which would you term cultural values? Do you agree or disagree with them in this case? Why?

SPORTS

Jim Willis is the principal of St. Mark's High School. Recently he fired the football coach who struck a player and tried to cover up the incident by asking other players to lie. Now the Boosters Club is threatening to withhold its contribution to the equipment fund unless Mr. Willis reinstates the coach. They feel that the coach's long winning record is important to the school's reputation and that the incident itself is understandable in a violent sport like football.

The money which is necessary to running the football program will have to come out of the general budget if the contribution is withheld by the Boosters. This will mean cutting either staff or academic programs.

What values are in conflict here? Which would you term cultural values? Do you agree or disagree with them in this case? Why?

FAMILY FEUD

Joe Antonelli is twenty-one and he has already worked two years for a large automobile manufacturer. His father, Gino, works in the same plant and is a vigorous member of the United Auto Workers. Gino remembers with pride his early years on the job. During the thirties, he had participated in the UAW struggles to get union bargaining power and benefits for workers. Now, forty years later, Gino gets a comfortable salary. He has a pleasant suburban home and two cars in his double garage. Besides putting in a good forty hours a week, Gino often works an extra sixteen on weekends. The extra money gives Gino a chance to make major improvements in his home.

His son never works overtime. In fact, Joe's record of absenteeism is an embarrassment to his father. The two men fight often. Gino says that Joe is irresponsible, lazy, and that a good day's work never hurt anyone. Joe says that his job is driving him crazy. He finds the assembly line routine deadening, the constant supervision annoying, and the lack of stimulation depressing. Joe wants "out"!

What values are in conflict here? Which would you term cultural values? Do you agree or disagree with them in this case? Why?

THEIR FEATS SHOW IT?

The search committee at Larson University has come up with

four candidates for a teaching position in the English department. The job description is for a teacher in modern poetry.

1) The first candidate, a highly respected poet, has not finished his Ph.D. requirements.

2) Another candidate is near retirement but has excellent credentials and a very fine teaching record.

3) The next candidate has fine credentials but is messy, even offensive in dress and personal hygiene.

4) The last candidate comes well-recommended as a poised, aggressive grant-getter.

What values are in conflict here? Which would you term cultural values? Do you agree or disagree with them in this case? Why?

A DIFFICULT CHOICE

Ms. Walters has been told recently by her daughter that she is pregnant. Further, her daughter intends to have an abortion in order not to jeopardize her college scholarship in music. Ms. Walters is convinced that abortion is wrong, but her daughter informs her that she has been counseled about her legal rights and is taking the decision into her own hands.

What values are in conflict here? Which would you term cultural values? Do you agree or disagree with them in this case? Why?

A WORLD OF TWO

Look over the photo essay on the following pages and ask yourself the same questions mentioned in the previous cases:

What values are in conflict here? Which would you term cultural values? Do you agree or disagree with them in this case? Why?

2 Our Reactions to Change

When media messages and friendly advice and conflicts like the ones described above come flying at us from all directions, we sense the great complexity of life. Behind all these specific issues, we sense *change* itself. Today's products and heroes and songs are gone tomorrow. Through the media we are aware immediately of swerving public opinion, of upheavals in the marketplace and in governments. The suddenness of change can easily make us feel threatened.

In fear we might find ourselves acting out of one of the limited perspectives described in an earlier chapter. Like **spectators,** we might act as if life and change are too complicated and messy to deal with. Like **conformists,** we might pretend we can control change entirely. Like **isolationists,** we might ignore change and decide instead "to do our own thing." Like **profiteers,** we might act as if taking care of "Number One" is all that matters.

We do not have to be intimidated by change, however. Although our decisions are finally our responsibility, we do not have to make them all on our own. We belong to the community of Church among whom are our parents and others who might gladly share their experience and advice. And we belong to communities which include other people of goodwill. Among all of us, the spirit of Jesus is at work enabling us to share and shape human history.

We are particularly fortunate if we have a *mentor* to help us in our life journey. Such a trusted counselor does not do our struggling for us but, by sharing his or her wealth of personal experience, a mentor encourages us to reach toward our full human potential in choosing our lifestyles and careers.

Bill Kaiser was fortunate in having such a mentor. In a physics class at a large university, Bill was one of 200 students taking the introductory course. Talbert Stein, his professor, was an excellent teacher who enjoyed being with his students. Despite his heavy teach-

ing and research load, Stein gave generously of time and talent by staying around after class to answer questions and to talk. Kaiser stayed too. Stein's fresh point of view and creative approach to physics led Kaiser to volunteer to work with Stein in the lab. Two and one-half years later, Kaiser was still there, richer in self-confidence and enthusiasm, and richer too in knowledge of physics and technical competency. The relationship between the two men grew to be one of real friendship as they car-pooled to the university each day, sharing experiences, disappointments, and hopes. Gradually Stein had become Bill's mentor.

The years passed and Kaiser graduated with a degree in physics. His work with Stein was invaluable experience for him personally; it was also an excellent apprenticeship that prepared him to do physics research with a major auto company. Looking back, Kaiser sees the tremendous impact that Stein has had in his life. His life direction and focus are due in large part to the influence of his excellent teacher and good friend, his mentor. What Bill admires most of all is Stein's ability to combine a life of care and concern for people with a career in research. Since Bill too plans a career in research, Stein's example stands as a continuing challenge and an inspiration.

Even with the help of mentors and people of goodwill and our church communities, it is difficult to know if we are following God's ways. How do we know? Summarizing what we have already said about decisions, sound judgment, prayer and discernment, much of the answer is contained in this excerpt from *How Do I Know I'm Doing Right?* by Gerard Sloyan:

I know I'm doing right if I try to be pure in intention in all that I do—what Jesus called being "single-minded" (see Matthew 5:8).

I know I'm doing right if I consult the teaching of Jesus Christ, Lord of the church, in his own words in the New Testament, and Moses and the prophets whom Jesus relied on, and Paul and those other apostles who taught in Jesus' name.

I know I'm doing right when I consciously make my love for God through my concern for individuals (*this* man, *this* woman) the measuring-stick for every choice.

I know I'm doing right when I consult the church to help me resolve my conscience: its bishop-teachers, its theologians and religious thinkers, its holy and learned members of my own acquaintance. In all that I do, I mean to seek the counsel of the brotherhood of believers—not theirs alone but that of any person of goodwill.

I know I'm doing right when I remain faithful to my conscience, which I have done everything in my power to inform.

I know I'm doing right if I follow with care current debate on the great contemporary moral issues heavy with social implications, on which the church has not been able to make a final judgment. I am the church, and my brothers and sisters need my help in this just as I need theirs.

I know I'm doing right if I pray for the grace of God in all that I do.

I know I'm doing right if I conceive sorrow for my sinfulness and not only for my sins. I must confess my serious sins humbly and sincerely, neither withholding them nor excusing them.

I know I'm doing right if I ask the Holy Spirit to make me a creature of love, a loving person in the human family and in the church; cleaving to what is right, rejecting what is wrong without fear or favor or human respect. What the Spirit *can* do in me to conform me to Christ as a child of the Father, *that* I ask that He *do* do.

3 "What Can I Do?"

In the next chapters, some very serious issues will be studied from the perspective of our Christian journey toward justice. Growth toward our full potential includes growth in concern for others. With increasing compassion we look to the needs of those around us and ask "What can I do?"

Some needs are clear and immediate. Others are complex and long-range. When we take seriously Jesus' challenge to become more fully human ourselves by sharing and shaping human history with others, those complex, long-range needs take on an air of urgency. We begin to ask: What can I do so that all people can have adequate food to live full human lives? What can I do so that all people can enjoy the benefits of energy without fear of war over limited supplies? What can I do so that all people can enjoy the freshness and beauty of our world without the threat of impending doom?

Some people consider these as no-win problems with no effective solutions. They wonder how anything we do can possibly make a difference. Two points should be restated in reply to this nagging sense of limitation. One is to remind ourselves that we shape life subtly but surely in lives shared with those close to us. Whatever lifestyle or career we choose, in any relationship we enter, in any situation we find ourselves, we have an opportunity to realize our own human potential and to help others to do the same. This principle holds true equally for the help we might give a younger brother or sister with homework, for the student pursuing a line of discussion in class, and for the Secretary of the United Nations mediating some international disagreement.

The second reply involves belief in and patience toward our own growth. The Austrian poet Rainer Maria Rilke put it this way:

> Be patient toward all that is unsolved in your heart and try to love the questions themselves . . . Live the questions now. Perhaps you will gradually, without noticing it, live along some distant day into the answer.

The question we must come "to love," and ask ourselves frequently and prayerfully, is this: "What can I do to shape the world toward justice?" As long as we are willing to ask that question, we know that we are heading, however hesitantly and slowly, in the right direction.

REVIEW QUESTIONS

1) How are our perspectives and our values influenced by parents? friends? teachers? the media?

2) How do you determine if cultural values are good or bad for you? for society?

3) What cultural values are highlighted in each of the case studies given in this chapter? How do these values affect our life and work toward justice?

4) How do mentors help us in our life journey? What other kinds of people can be helpful to us, according to Gerard Sloyan?

5

Growth:
The Shape of Tomorrow

We travel together, passengers
on a little spaceship,
dependent on its vulnerable
reserves of air and soil . . .
preserved from annihilation
only by the care, the work,
and I will say the love
we give our fragile craft.

Adlai E. Stevenson

Growth is life's driving force. From the simplest to the most complex forms of life, everything must grow and develop. Most of the time growth is healthy. Sometimes growth is unhealthy. Unhealthy growth, chaotic and cancer-like, undermines life and leads to death.

What is true of natural life is analogously true of social life. Societies too grow and develop. Society's growth can be permeated with a drive toward justice and full human life, or it can be fraught with alienation, injustice, and death.

History shows unparalleled growth in population, industrial production, and pollution since World War II. This growth can be a positive and life-giving force for justice in the world, or it can be a negative and death-dealing excuse for injustice. The choice is ours. Will we watch or approve as the chasm of injustice and alienation widens? Will we seize every opportunity for personal gain? Or will we work toward kinship, justice, and full human life for everyone?

The quality of society's growth is reflected in all levels but especially in its institutions. Economic, political, cultural, and religious institutions serve society's healthy growth when they respond to society's real needs. Those same institutions undermine society's healthy growth when they seek only their own survival and profit.

Our major decisions, that is, the careers we choose and the lifestyles we adopt, can shape the institutions of society and so determine the quality of its growth. To make those decisions effectively we must examine the dynamics of growth within a broad time and space perspective, and discover how our personal and collective decisions can direct that growth toward justice for all people.

1 Population Growth

Reasons for the unprecedented population growth of the past half century are both simple and complex. How we perceive and understand that growth depends very much on where we live in this world and on our fundamental perspective, that is, our way of looking at the world.

Some people in wealthy nations look at rapid population growth in poor nations and blame the poor nations' food and resource problems on that growth. Their counterparts in poor nations look at the same rapid population growth and blame food and resource problems on wasteful use of those resources by wealthy nations. When we see population growth from these two different perspectives, it is not surprising if we reach different conclusions and make different decisions.

HISTORICAL FACTS

No matter where we live or how broad our time and space viewpoint, our examination of the dynamics of population growth must be rooted in historical facts if we hope to weigh options and to choose future directions effectively.

Global population is the total number of people living in the world at a given time. Population increases through the centuries are due to the difference between the number of births and the number of deaths. Global population becomes a *problem* when people's most basic physical and safety needs cannot be met. In this case, they live on the lower rungs of Maslow's ladder, with little time or energy to be concerned about problems beyond those immediate needs.

The following chart illustrates some of the differences between developing and developed countries. Some people explain this disparity between the "haves" and the "have nots," the rich and the poor, by saying that there are just too many people in the world. They say that it is impossible for everyone to have enough food, water, and basic security. Whether or not we agree with this

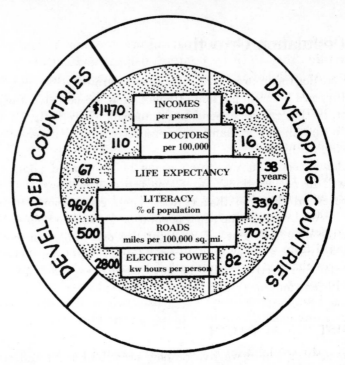

DEVELOPED COUNTRIES

DEVELOPING COUNTRIES

$1470	INCOMES per person	$130
110	DOCTORS per 100,000	16
67 years	LIFE EXPECTANCY	38 years
96%	LITERACY % of population	33%
500	ROADS miles per 100,000 sq. mi.	70
2800	ELECTRIC POWER kw hours per person	82

HANDICAPS OF DEVELOPING COUNTRIES. This figure shows that the advantages enjoyed by many people in developed countries are not available to many others who live in developing countries.

assessment, two facts emerge with increasing urgency: (1) the social and economic needs that plague poor countries are accentuated by increasing numbers of people; (2) wealthy countries bask in affluence and gobble up resources that could be used to meet those needs.

To better understand how this situation came about, we should examine the growth and decline of human populations. This is called demographic history. Its broad outline reveals four periods:

1) **before the discovery of agriculture.**
2) **from the discovery of agriculture to the beginning of the Industrial Revolution.**
3) **from the Industrial Revolution to World War II.**
4) **from World War II to the present.**

1) Before the discovery of agriculture, the human family was **nomadic.** They lived by hunting, fishing, and gathering wild fruits. As individuals they rarely rose above the first and most basic levels of human needs. We can only speculate on populations during this period, but to have survived for any length of time in such a precarious way of life, high fertility probably balanced high mortality rates.

2) With the discovery of agriculture about twelve thousand years ago, people began to grow food and domesticate animals. Since they no longer had to leave an area to search for food, they could settle in more permanent locations. Gradually, as they changed from a nomadic to an **agrarian** lifestyle, demographic patterns changed too. People suffered sudden peaks of death rates due to epidemics, famines, other natural disasters, and wars. By A.D. 1750, as agriculture was giving way to industrialization, there were about 750 million people on the Earth.

3) **Industrialization** began slowly, around the middle of the eighteenth century. It created new economic opportunities and possibilities for advances in technical and scientific knowledge which in turn accelerated population growth. More infants survived and more people lived to old age. By 1940, the world population had risen to over two billion.

4) Our present period began about the time of World War II. Vast amounts of government spending for military needs produced civilian benefits. As a result, scientific ingenuity, economic activity and opportunities lowered death rates dramatically. Birth rates remained unchanged for a time and population growth was phenomenal. A recent world census has placed total world population at over four billion. This large-scale and rapid growth has sometimes been called "the population explosion."

In earlier ages, food, energy, and other resources exceeded the demand for them, so population growth was of little consequence. Now that has changed. Today we live in a world of increasing

interdependence, where the consequences of continuing population growth affect everyone. Making the world's resources available to all people is the challenging task of imagineers in all parts of the world and in every walk of life.

DEVELOPING NATIONS

Two-thirds of the people in the world live in traditional, agrarian economies of developing countries, not unlike the second period of demographic history just described. Life is hard and basic needs frequently are unmet. Life for these people is often a daily scramble to provide the bare minimum of food, clothing, and shelter for themselves and their families. And yet, these are the people whose numbers are growing rapidly.

Historically, the lowering of birth rates is directly related to substantial improvements in the standard of living. Britain, Japan, and the United States attest to the fact that when economic development reaches the majority of people, population growth tends to stabilize, even decline. Furthermore, history shows that:

1) When nutrition improves, when water is readily available, when sanitation and health care needs are met, fewer children die and people live longer.

2) When people have some basic education, they begin to plan their lives and their families.

3) When people's incomes improve, they can purchase food and other basic necessities.

4) When pensions and social security are readily available, people do not have to depend exclusively on children for economic support in illness and old age.

In an attempt to lower birth rates, leaders in some developing countries have established national population objectives. Realizing these objectives, however, seems to be an almost impossible

SOCIETY IS UNABLE
TO PROVIDE PEOPLES'
BASIC NEEDS

INDIVIDUALS HAVE
MORE CHILDREN
TO OFFSET HIGHER
MORTALITY RATE

INDIVIDUALS VALUE
CHILDREN AS ECONOMIC
SUPPORT AND SECURITY

POVERTY AND
MALNUTRITION FURTHER
STRAIN SOCIETY'S CAPABILITIES—
CHILDREN DIE AT INCREASING RATE

PEOPLE-POVERTY CYCLE.

feat since many people disagree profoundly with their government's policies. Despite serious ramifications beyond those of the immediate family, they say that having children is an intensely personal matter, not to be dictated by the state. Consequently, leaders in developing countries continue to establish population objectives, people continue to ignore them, and the number of people in those countries continues to rise. Meeting the basic needs for food and safety of rapidly rising populations remains a serious problem.

What might seem to be simply a *population* problem in developing countries is, at root, a *poverty* problem. Increasing numbers make it more difficult for people to meet their needs for food, employment, education, and health care, but increasing numbers alone are not the *cause* of these problems. Parents in developing countries desperately need children, especially sons, both to work the land and to care for them in old age. In situations of high infant mortality, this inevitably leads to high birth rates. Thus the people-poverty cycle continues.

From the perspective of justice, this people-poverty cycle is intolerable on several counts:

1) It undermines the family, the foundation of society.

2) It deprives great numbers of persons of the basic means necessary for full human life.

3) It widens the chasm between wealthy and poor nations.

4) It perpetuates systems (institutions) fraught with alienation and injustice.

This people-poverty cycle *can* be broken. It *will* be broken when our personal and collective decisions stem from a broad framework and penetrate all levels of society with works of justice. *The key to healthy population growth lies not in preventing life anywhere in the world, but in enhancing it everywhere.*

Alice Hamilton
Physician, Pioneer in Industrial Medicine

Outside of marriage there were few careers open to women in the latter part of the nineteenth century. Alice Hamilton was a fiercely independent woman however; she had other ideas.

By the age of twenty-four, Hamilton had already earned a medical degree from the University of Michigan. As a young doctor she moved to Chicago, to a neighborhood of dilapidated tenements, poorly ventilated factories and smelting plants. Her new life as a professional in such surroundings contrasted sharply with earlier days in her family's comfortable home in Fort Wayne and with school days at a private girls' academy.

In Chicago, she regularly saw men working in clouds of lead-laden dust, inhaling fumes from oxide furnaces and eating their meager lunches in the midst of those fumes. It was an atmosphere of death and Hamilton knew it. Many of her neighbors were immigrants who had worked in the same mills, factories, and foundries, and breathed the same kinds of fumes. Then the day came when they could no longer work—they were invalids.

Dogged determination led this slender, tweed-clad woman to tramp the streets of Chicago's slums and track down actual cases of lead poisoning. That same determination led her to convince industry's leaders to provide good building ventilation and better working conditions. By 1915, Alice Hamilton was *the* recognized expert on lead poisoning in the United States. Her work in industrial medicine paved the way for Illinois lawmakers to pass this country's first workmen's compensation law.

Throughout her long and vigorous life, Alice Hamilton was happy and never forgot what her mother once said, "There are two kinds of people in the world, the ones who say, 'Somebody ought to do something about that, but why should I?' and those who say, 'Somebody must do something about that, then why not I?' "

DEVELOPED NATIONS

Roughly one-third of the people in the world live in the industrialized nations of Europe and North America. Compared with our counterparts in the rest of the world, life is easier and basic needs are often taken for granted. Ours is not a people-poverty cycle, but an abundance-waste boom with important implications for population growth.

Any serious effort to raise the standard of living of the world's poor means that people in wealthy nations can no longer enjoy certain advantages at the expense of those in poor nations. However, people in wealthy, industrialized nations are using increasing amounts of resources per person. While population increases very little, consumption of resources climbs steadily. We live a throwaway lifestyle which one writer describes this way:

> **Americans are unique in the way they think, speak, act and treat one another. When we walk down the streets of London or Paris, the English or the French know we are Americans, even before we open our mouths or wave a credit card. Our uniqueness is connected with our consumption habits, the way we spend, exploit and discard material things. We are captivated by telephones and superhighways; we drive powerful and bulky cars; we supercool or superheat our homes; we drink hot coffee with cold ice cream. Consumption is America's obsession.**

At the root of this obsession may be a scramble for safety and security, hoping that these things will fill our needs or move us a step higher on Maslow's ladder. It may be a jostling for independence, esteem, or respect. Whatever its roots, this obsession is not unique to present-day North Americans. In 1877, Chief Sitting Bull described some of our ancestors:

> **Yet, hear me, people, we have now to deal with another race, small and feeble when our fathers first met them but now great and overbearing. Strangely enough,**

they have a mind to till the soil and the love of possession is a disease with them.

Love of possessions and lifestyles based in consumerism are fed by institutions whose exclusive end is profit. These institutions have no concern for society's real needs. By advertising unnecessary luxuries as "needs," they undermine society's healthy growth.

Some Americans are tiring of affluent, wasteful lifestyles and are choosing lives of voluntary simplicity. This break away from the values of consumerism and waste can be a move toward concern for those beyond our national boundaries and for future generations. It can also be a cumulative recognition that our

EMPHASIS IN CONSUMERISM WORLD VIEW	EMPHASIS IN SIMPLICITY WORLD VIEW
Values	*Values*
Material growth	Material sufficiency coupled with psycho-spiritual growth
Conquest of nature	Stewardship of nature
Competitive self-interest	Enlightened self-interest
Rugged individualism	Cooperative individualism
Social Characteristics	*Social Characteristics*
Large, complex living and working environments	Smaller, less complex living and working environments
Space-age technology	Appropriate technology
Identity defined by patterns of consumption	Identity found through inner and interpersonal discovery
Mass produced, quickly obsolete, standarized products	Hand crafted, durable, unique products
High pressure, rat race existence	Relaxed, more human existence

This figure contrasts some of the differences between lifestyles based on consumerism and lifestyles based on the values of voluntary simplicity. Adapted from Elgin and Mitchell, "Voluntary Simplicity: Life-Style of the Future?" *The Futurist*, August 1977.

needs for safety, love, and esteem can never be fulfilled by hoarding or spending. Without proper motivation, it could also be a flight from the challenges of industrialization and a denial of responsible use of talents.

Career and lifestyle decisions based on the values of voluntary simplicity are significantly different from those based on consumerism. When we live and work in voluntary simplicity, we can lessen the strain on Earth's resources and establish a better balance between population and resources. We can grow to see ourselves more truly as members of a global society living in a broad perspective. Seventeenth century poet John Donne put it this way:

> **No man is an island,**
> **entire of itself;**
> **every man is a piece of the continent**
> **a part of the main . . .**
> **any man's death diminishes me,**
> **because I am involved in mankind . . .**

A life of voluntary simplicity involves honest assessment of our personal talents, needs, and values. It involves critical, ongoing assessment of the role and use of material goods in our lives. And it involves ongoing decisions and actions to maximize human well-being and to minimize waste of human talent and natural resources. Human judgment and prayerful discernment can be very helpful in choosing a lifestyle of voluntary simplicity.

In *Justice in the World,* the Synod of Bishops challenged Christians in these words:

> **It must be asked whether belonging to the Church places people on a rich island within an ambient of poverty. In societies enjoying a higher level of consumer spending, it must be asked whether our lifestyle exemplifies the sparingness with regard to consumption which we preach to others as necessary in order that so many millions of hungry people throughout the world may be fed (#48).**

2 Growth in Industrialization

From the dawn of civilization, people have needed certain material goods in order to meet basic physical and safety needs. These needs increase as society becomes more complex. People of one age build on the knowledge, discoveries, and technologies of their predecessors. Today, historians of technology can trace how one invention led to another and how these in turn led to still greater inventions, thus increasing industrial production enormously. Modern industrialization and technology have made possible the production of goods that were only imagined in earlier days. Today's enormous capacity for production can have a positive impact on people everywhere when the profits of production are more equitably distributed. Even today, however, some people still lack the minimum of goods necessary for life and safety.

DEVELOPING NATIONS

Most people in developing countries still live in *pre-industrial, agrarian* economies where they use nearly all their energies to provide the necessities of life. Many scratch out a bare subsistence on small patches of land. Others mine the raw materials for industrial development, but they themselves do not benefit from that development. For them, modern industrialization and its accompanying economic welfare are still in the future.

One of the ways that poor countries can boost their economic welfare is to engage in trade. World trade is a very complex issue involving tariffs, quotas, balance of payments, and other political considerations. To understand some of this complexity, we should examine a few examples.

Some developing countries supply industrialized nations with the raw materials necessary for industrial production. Other developing countries supply cash crops grown primarily for trade. Industrialized nations, in turn, supply developing countries with manufactured goods.

Developing countries are generally small-scale suppliers to the world market, so they have little say about the price of goods. With certain notable exceptions, like oil, the prices of unprocessed, raw materials have not kept pace with the prices of manufactured goods. This fact makes the relationship between industrialized nations and developing countries one of unequal partners. Marketing demands or cartel decisions have also made prices fluctuate widely. Exceptionally sharp price rises followed by sudden drops make realistic economic planning and growth exceedingly difficult in many developing countries. The following chart illustrates the substantial price variations encountered in the global marketplace.

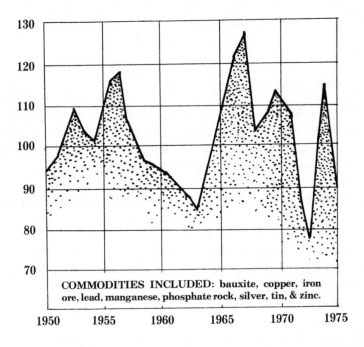

COMMODITIES INCLUDED: bauxite, copper, iron ore, lead, manganese, phosphate rock, silver, tin, & zinc.

PRICE VARIATIONS OF NINE MINERALS EXPORTED FROM DEVELOPING COUNTRIES, 1950-1975. This figure illustrates price variations that make economic planning in developing countries very difficult (Source: Sewell, et. al., *The United States and World Development Agenda, 1977*).

Developing countries that export food are particularly vulnerable to price changes and resulting economic chaos. Countries like Ghana whose chief export is cocoa, or Kenya whose chief export is tea and coffee, find that world demand for their goods is growing slower than world demand for industrial raw materials which other countries offer. As their demand for manufactured goods increases with population growth, the gap between them and the rest of the world widens.

Developing countries that export raw materials are in a better trading position because industrialized nations need increasing amounts of those resources for continued growth in production. Sometimes these developing countries can join together and raise prices for their goods on the world market. The Organization of Petroleum Exporting Countries (OPEC) is one example.

If developing countries are going to make the transition from traditional, agrarian economies to more modern industrial ones, they need to make decisions that further economic development in ways uniquely suited to their situations. Decisions of how to further that economic development must be carefully weighed. For a long time, economic development meant transplanting technology from the wealthy nations of Europe and North America to the poor nations of Asia, Africa, and Latin America. Development meant imitation. Fortunately, that view is changing.

Poor countries that have slipped or been pushed into decisions that imitate the production and consumption patterns of wealthy nations now find themselves locked into sophisticated technology which keeps many people poor and unemployed and concentrates wealth in the hands of a few. Those decisions are counterproductive and even somewhat comical as shown by the following example.

An African textile mill was operating at one of the highest technological levels possible. Since African

laborers were unused to industrial work, they made poor production workers. In a first attempt to eliminate the human factor, the manager decided to import his equipment from the most advanced countries. This sophisticated equipment then necessitated importing management and maintenance personnel. Before it was over, even raw materials had to be imported because the locally grown cotton was too short for top quality yarn!

Instead of transplanting the sophisticated but inappropriate technology of developed countries, imaginative, resourceful leaders in developing countries are encouraging the use of technology that is appropriate to local needs, skills, and resources. This kind of technology is on a smaller scale, more labor intensive (that is, provides jobs for more people instead of replacing them with machines), and more directed toward meeting the needs of all rather than the wants of a few. Such technology does not just happen. It is the result of sound, effective decisions.

Decision makers on both sides of the wealthy-poor chasm incorporate talents, needs, and values into their major decisions. However different those talents, needs, and values may be, the process of decision-making remains essentially the same. First, we gather a reasonable amount of information and interpret that information as thoroughly and objectively as possible. Then, from among a number of possible alternatives, we choose one course of action, implement the decision by appropriate action, and evaluate the decision in light of its effects. A few examples demonstrate.

SRI LANKA

Hubert Fernando is from Sri Lanka, an island of almost thirteen million people off the southern tip of India. Rice is the staple crop. For many years the Sri Lankans had processed their rice with technology transplanted from industrialized nations—technology

fired by oil or electricity and involving several processes. Fernando worked with the Department of
Agriculture, so he had ample opportunity to gather
information about rice processing. He assessed the
situation and began to wonder if there could be a *better*
way. Different scenarios suggested themselves as he
asked, "What would happen if . . . ?"

One day he held a lighted cigarette to a grain of
unhusked rice and discovered that direct heat could
simplify rice processing considerably. He chose to
pursue that discovery and for more than a decade of
trial and error worked to invent a machine that would
provide an alternative way to process rice. Sheer determination led to the breakthrough and the invention
of a processing machine many times smaller than the
conventional one. Fernando's machine operates on an
entirely different principle, and perhaps its greatest
genius is its near-zero fuel costs. The energy that
drives it comes from burning the husk from the rice.
Fernando's invention could drive into obsolescence

the standard Western technology for rice processing. It could increase Asian rice production, reduce energy costs, and free Asia from dependence on more expensive, sophisticated technology.

KENYA

Aston Manyindo is another effective imagineer. As UNICEF's director of village technology at the Karen, Kenya Institute in East Africa, Manyindo gathers information about appropriate technology from many parts of the developing world. He demonstrates a machine from South America that mixes earth and cement to make cheap and durable bricks; from China, a water lifting device based on a 2,000-year-old design; and from Tanzania, a bicycle-powered maise sheller.

GREAT BRITAIN

O. G. Thomas is yet another imaginative decision maker. Thomas is founder of Anti-Poverty, a British organization which helps young people to become better informed about world development by making their own useful and practical contribution to it. Thomas enlisted the expertise of young technicians at Rolls Royce Technical College to design and to put together machinery and low cost technology to meet particular needs in developing countries. Prior to any effective action, the young technicians gathered and interpreted information about needs and resources. For this they employed a young engineer who had just returned from several years overseas. Then, from among many options, they chose to produce an inexpensive device for hardening steel, a simple pump for pumping water out of catchment tanks, a press to extract oil from oil seeds, and a solar waterheating system.

Decision makers like Fernando, Manyindo, and Thomas hasten the day when the world's poor will share the profits of production. Each in his own way unites human imagination and a technological bent into a vital force of creative energy. Each in his own way strives to raise his personal decisions to a social or community level so that their impact can more effectively serve the real needs of society.

DEVELOPED NATIONS

Most people in developed nations live with certain benefits of the Industrial Age. Life is easier, and, if judged by material standards alone, better. Industrialization, however, has had a high price. Many modern industrial people no longer see themselves as part of nature. Instead, they see themselves *above* nature and so try to exploit and dominate it. The result is alienation.

Some people suggest that industrialized nations have so exploited Earth's limited resources that we cannot possibly continue to survive in this affluent lifestyle, nor can we help pre-industrialized nations to reach even a modest standard of living. This is hard for some North Americans to understand.

Past industrial development has been based on the availability of plentiful and cheap resources. We are slowly recognizing that our rapid industrial development and economic expansion have been based on the myth of inexhaustibility. Recent oil and gas shortages have exploded that myth. We can now recognize that the supplies that made industrialization possible are limited. However vast they may be, they are *not* inexhaustible. Petroleum, coal, natural gas, and the metals found in the Earth's crust can be discovered, but once used, they are gone forever.

Our North American lifestyle uses enormous amounts of these nonrenewable resources. As these become less available worldwide, they become more costly. Soon only wealthy nations will be able to afford them. But world demand is growing. The following chart illustrates how much more of these resources would be

RUBBER

**WOULD BE CONSUMED
AT 5.7 TIMES
THE PRESENT WORLD
LEVEL.**

TIN

**WOULD BE CONSUMED
AT 4.5 TIMES
THE PRESENT WORLD
LEVEL.**

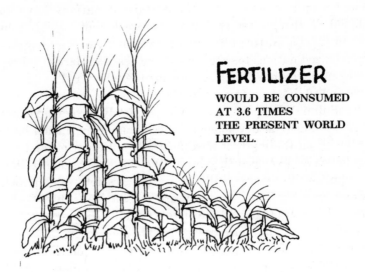

FERTILIZER

**WOULD BE CONSUMED
AT 3.6 TIMES
THE PRESENT WORLD
LEVEL.**

IF THE WORLD CONSUMED AT CURRENT U.S. ANNUAL LEVEL
(Source: United Nations).

needed if people in other countries consumed at the current U.S. level.

In quantitative terms, the bulk of expanding world consumption is in rich nations like the United States. When increased consumption becomes the ultimate goal of an individual or a society, it imprisons, restricts, and binds that individual or society. Expedience and self-interest govern personal and collective decisions. Rather than promoting kinship, justice, and full human life through the equitable use of resources, those decisions entrap people and perpetuate alienation and injustice.

Men and women who hold responsible positions in industries and corporations have crucial responsibilities in this regard. Their decisions can waste or conserve resources. They can allow corporations to produce more luxury goods for an already affluent society, or they can prompt those corporations to produce more moderate goods to meet the needs of a larger number of people.

All of us need a minimum of material goods in order to meet basic physical and safety needs. Personal and collective decisions governed by profit motives and self-interest widen the chasm between the wealthy, industrialized nations and the poor, agrarian ones. Those decisions make it more difficult for people in poor nations to have the minimum of material goods necessary for full human life.

On the other hand, personal and collective decisions governed by a sense of service and justice narrow the chasm and make it possible for all people to reach a modest standard of living.

We can develop a perspective that sees beyond national boundaries and extends into the future. We can shape our own lives and society's institutions by our career and lifestyle decisions. By these decisions we can more equitably share the profits of production and so carry out the works of justice.

In *Justice in the World,* the Synod of Bishops put the issue into these terms:

It is impossible to see what right the richer nations have to keep up their claim to increase their own mate-

rial demands, if the consequence is either that others remain in misery or that the danger of destroying the very physical foundations of life on earth is precipitated. Those who are already rich are bound to accept a less material way of life, with less waste, in order to avoid the destruction of the heritage which they are obliged by justice to share with all other members of the human race (#70).

3 Growth in Pollution

Industrialization highlights the disparity between the wealthy and poor people of our planet; pollution highlights the disruption between ourselves and our environment. Disruption of the environment is not unique to modern times. Nomadic herdsmen and hunters as far back as the Stone Age burned down forests and overgrazed grasslands. Compared with the impact of industrialization, however, past transgressions, whether deliberate or accidental, fade into insignificance. The disruption of the environment in this twentieth century is more far-reaching, more deadly, than in previous generations.

Adlai E. Stevenson once described the Earth as an isolated island of life with a closed life-support system much like that of a spacecraft. That image is no illusion. Our world is a marvelous complexity of living things, an interdependent web of life-giving cycles of incredible delicacy and diversity. But it is fragile. When we live in ways that ignore or scorn its fragility, we court disaster.

"Pollution" conjures up negative images: dirty streams and rivers, sooty air, chemicals added to food, DDT, oil spills, uncollected garbage . . . Even the most useful substances, however, can become pollutants. Even natural substances in concentrated levels and in the wrong places can be harmful and even deadly. Insulin and sugar are examples. Insulin is a natural, organic substance which enables the body to use and to store sugar. When the body does not produce enough insulin, sugar builds up in (and pollutes) the blood. When the body produces too much insulin (a polluting level), the blood does not contain enough sugar. In both cases, the person suffers fatigue, headache, and nervousness. If left untreated, either condition can eventually lead to death.

Many pollutants are not natural, organic substances like insulin and sugar. Some pollutants are wholly new substances, the result of people's collective ingenuity and imagineering skills. Since scientists have learned how to take molecules apart and put them together in new ways, we have a whole array of synthetics: plastics, detergents, fibers, rubber, insecticides, and fertilizers. These new substances are based on postwar production technologies and differ significantly from natural, organic substances. Replacing natural, organic products with synthetic ones can cause environmental stress and add a new dimension to the problem of pollution.

TRAGEDY IN JAPAN

Minamata, Japan, illustrates the tragic results of environmental pollution. Until the early 1900s, Minamata was a quiet, pre-industrial community in southern Japan. Its large, nearly landlocked bay with a steady supply of nourishment and trade was a fisherman's haven. Then, in 1907, village leaders convinced the founder of a company that would later become the Chisso Corporation to build a factory in their town, and Minamata joined the industrial age. Forty years later, Chisso was a leading producer of petrochemicals and plastics, and Minamata was a thriving factory town of about 40,000 people.

Those people began to feel an eerie uneasiness in the early 1950s when fish floated on the water's surface and birds dropped into the sea. Other animals acted strange, then died. Finally, a little girl, unable to walk, incoherent in speech, and suffering severe delirium,

entered the factory's hospital. She became the first
recognized case of "Minamata Disease"—the first of
many. Once-healthy men and women suffered violent
convulsions which left them crippled and helpless.
Babies of seemingly healthy mothers were afflicted
even before birth.

The mysterious "disease" reached epidemic proportions before research groups finally pinpointed the
cause: irreversible mercury poisoning originating in
Chisso's industrial waste and dumped into the bay. As
the mercury moved up the food chain, it became more
concentrated until it finally reached toxic levels in the
fish which was food for the villagers. Chisso had
poisoned Minamata's waters, the aquatic food chain,
and eventually a great number of men, women, and
children.

Unfortunately, no effective decisions were made to
stop or to treat the flow of industrial waste into the bay
until it was too late. Fear, expediency, and greed governed decisions by Chisso's management. Their too

narrow time and space perspective caused them to manipulate, cheat, lie, and forge documents in an attempt to escape responsibility. Finally, in 1973, after a long legal battle between the corporation and the townspeople, Chisso was declared legally responsible for the pollution that was causing mercury poisoning to destroy its victims' central nervous systems. Two years later, Chisso had paid indemnities totaling more than eighty million dollars.

The real tragedy of Minamata, however, is its human cost. By 1975, more than 800 victims had been verified, and another 2,800 applicants were waiting for verification.

These events at Minamata reach beyond the individuals involved. They urge all of us to take seriously the interdependence of life on this planet and to make decisions accordingly. They urge us to take seriously the task of gathering a reasonable amount of information and interpreting that information thoroughly and objectively. They urge us to consider alternatives carefully, to think about "What would happen if. . .?" and to take appropriate action. Equally important, the events at Minamata urge us to examine personal needs and values and to see the impact those needs and values can have at a social or community level.

EVERYBODY'S PROBLEM

Global capacity to absorb pollutants is very great, but as Minamata attests, local overloading can lead to human tragedy. People who live in the large cities of the world experience local overloading through dirtier air and murkier water. By the year 2000, it is estimated that six out of every ten people in the world will live in cities. As more people crowd into urban areas they generate ever greater amounts of pollution and are exposed to diseases directly linked to pollution.

A broad perspective will not permit any person, municipality, or industry to degrade the resources of air, water, and land that we share in common. People, municipalities, and industries can work for the preservation, wise use, and equitable distribution of those resources. By our personal and collective decisions we can develop policies that use Earth's resources well, serve society's real needs, and effectively humanize our lives and our cities.

As we grow to appreciate our power to shape history by our personal and collective decisions, we need to take a closer look at our talents, needs, and values. These are the tools and motivating forces we bring to decision-making. We can recognize talents and work to develop them; recognize needs and try to meet them; recognize values and deepen or reorder them.

Some people have the talent and inclination to work on the problems of pollution. They can choose careers as biologists, chemists, engineers, farmers, medical researchers, or leaders in industry. Other people have the talent and inclination to care for those who suffer the results of pollution. They can choose careers as nurses, doctors, therapists, and paramedical workers. Others have the talent and inclination to work for health and safety measures in their homes, neighborhoods, schools or in the shops, factories, mines, or buildings where they work. Each person's talents are important. Joined with others, our talents are powerful tools that can change society's institutions to deal effectively with environmental issues.

Not everyone will choose a career that works on problems of pollution, but everyone can choose a lifestyle of voluntary simplicity, one that respects nature and looks to the welfare of future generations. One of the values implicit in voluntary simplicity is ecological awareness, that is, a sense of the interdependence between people and resources. This awareness enables us to learn from the past, to deal with the present, and to shape the future. It enables us to imagineer a future that is just and worthy to be called human. Some of its concrete expressions might include supporting political candidates who want to deal with environmental issues, joining community or neighborhood ecology groups, or helping to mobilize against local pollution through social, political, or legal action. More immediate concrete expressions might include decisions to avoid aerosol sprays, plastic wrapped foods, and throwaway bottles or cans, and to buy, instead, conditioners and cleaners that are used in liquid or solid forms, fresh food and produce that does not require packaging, and milk and other beverages in returnable bottles or cans. Ecological awareness also enables us to become less car-dependent, to realize that walking and biking are good exercise and that they save energy and money and lessen pollutants in the air.

Ecological awareness does not just "happen." It demands gathering pertinent information and interpreting that information as thoroughly and objectively as we can. These first two steps of decision-making prepare us to weigh options and to choose effective careers and lifestyles.

4 Measuring Growth

If the United States economy grows by five percent in a given year, this does not mean that the quality of life in the United States is five percent better than the previous year. If the average North American is twenty times wealthier than the average Bolivian, this does not mean that North America is twenty times better as a place to live. Measuring growth by the belief that "bigger and more equals better" could lead us to value *maximum* consumption. Measuring growth by the underlying respect for nature and the long-range concern for the welfare of future generations leads us to evaluate growth differently — as *optimal* consumption.

Contrasting these two views—*maximum* consumption and *optimum* consumption—E. F. Schumacher stated that by definition optimum consumption would take less effort to achieve. He added:

> **We need not be surprised, therefore, that the pressure and strain of living is very much less in, say, Burma than it is in the United States in spite of the fact that the amount of labor-saving machinery used in the former is only a minute fraction of the amount used in the latter.**

The traditional measure of economic growth in any country is its **gross national product.** GNP is the total value of all consumption and investment goods plus government expenditures on goods and services. To chart a nation's growth by its rising GNP is to have some picture of that country's economic progress. It is only a partial picture, however.

Growth statistics that seem most impressive could actually be an illusion that allows us to drift into unwise, short-sighted decisions. Even when GNP takes inflation into account, using it as the sole measure of growth falls short on several counts:

E. F. Schumacher
Economist and Writer

Until recently, for most Americans "small is beautiful" had an unfamiliar ring. "Bigger is better" had long characterized modern Western thought. Then, in 1972, E. F. Schumacher, a British economist, published a collection of essays that captured the imagination of people around the world. *Small Is Beautiful* was translated into fifteen languages, became a world best seller, and vaulted Schumacher into the international limelight.

Schumacher's thesis was simple enough: no amount of comfort or wealth can compensate people for policies or structures that insult their self-respect and impair their freedom. To the profit-based economy he suggested an alternative, "economics as if people matter," that is, one with a moral basis.

Schumacher combined the wisdom found in Buddhism with the ideals of the Christian gospel and translated them into economic terms. He encouraged people in developing countries to reject the breakneck urbanization, mass production, centralized development planning, and advanced technology of Western development, and to choose instead to stabilize and to enrich their traditional ways of life. Using labor-intensive methods to manufacture goods and keeping their country's economic decision-making as decentralized as possible would build up a strong morale and build on people's desire to be self-determining.

When he died of an apparent stroke in Switzerland in the fall of 1977, this friendly-looking, white-haired man left this challenge: More and more people are beginning to realize that the modern experiment of living without religion has failed. They are beginning to look in the right direction. But will enough people do so quickly enough to save the modern world?

1) GNP is never equally distributed in society. Even a high average per capita GNP does not necessarily imply the well-being of large segments of society, since its actual distribution may be in very unequal proportions.

2) There is no automatic relationship between a rising GNP and fundamental improvements such as life expectancy, death rates, infant mortality, and literacy.

3) GNP can actually *increase* while the quality of life *decreases* because of pollution and ecological costs.

Although GNP will continue to be used as one measure of economic growth, additional criteria should be developed. The United Nations and others are working toward a supplement per capita GNP that measures progress toward meeting human needs.

We can assume that people everywhere want to live longer, to have their children live longer, and to have greater opportunity. A good composite index should therefore measure life expectancy, infant mortality, and literacy. It might even measure other social and psychological characteristics suggested in the term "quality of life." This type of measure has the advantage of measuring the *quality* as well as *quantity* of growth.

Industrialized nations generally score well on life expectancy, infant mortality, and literacy. Most of us have our basic physical needs met and are able to be concerned with what Maslow calls "higher" needs. As we grow in giving and receiving affection, in self-respect, independence, and personal inner strength, the quality of our lives changes. We become richer and in turn enrich society. Even in industrialized nations, however, especially in large cities, we see people who are unable to move beyond mere safety needs. Despite impressive growth statistics, the quality of life in industrialized nations stands in need of improvement when looked at in this perspective. Our personal and collective decisions will determine how that will come about.

When enough people make decisions that influence the quality of society's growth in a positive way, we can permeate society with a sense of kinship and justice. When enough Christians recognize Jesus' challenge to do the works of justice by sharing and shaping human history, we will choose careers and lifestyles that enhance the quality of life wherever we are and in whatever we do.

REVIEW QUESTIONS

1) How can our major decisions help to determine the quality of society's healthy growth?

2) Why is the population problem in developing countries basically a poverty problem?

3) What are the implications for population growth resulting from the "abundance-waste boom" in developed nations?

4) What kinds of changes are necessary in order that growth in industrial production can benefit all people?

5) Why is world trade such a complex issue?

6) Why is it counterproductive to transplant technology from the highly industrialized nations to the underdeveloped ones? What are some viable alternatives?

7) What is the "myth of inexhaustibility"? How has this myth affected cultural values in North America?

8) How does pollution highlight the disruption between ourselves and our environment?

9) What lessons can be learned from the tragedy at Minamata?

10) What is ecological awareness? In what ways are we all challenged to live and promote ecological awareness?

11) What is the difference between "maximum consumption" and "optimum consumption"? How does a concern for the quality of life affect our consumption, values, and decisions?

12) What are some careers and lifestyles that this chapter suggests to you?

6

Food:
Deciding Who Shall Eat

If everybody took enough
food for himself and no more,
there would be no pauperism,
there would be no man
dying of starvation
in this world.

Mahatma Gandhi

If Earth were a village of one hundred people, it would look something like this:

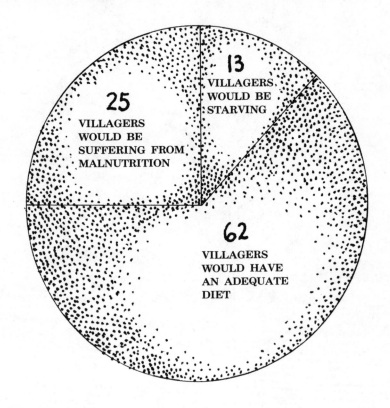

All the villagers have the same human needs described previously in Maslow's hierarchy. When our needs for food, water, and rest, for safety and security are at least somewhat satisfied, we can direct our efforts in service to others and toward justice for all people. When these basic needs are not satisfied, however, we are thwarted in our capacity for service and justice.

Our most basic need is food. In our hypothetical village of one hundred people, there is enough food for everyone to have an adequate diet. However, twenty-five wealthy people consume more grain than all the other seventy-five people put together. Meanwhile, hunger and starvation stalk thirteen villagers and another twenty-five would benefit from a more varied diet. Half of the child deaths in the village are attributable to malnutrition.

Actually, Earth is a village of more than four billion people. The United Nations estimates that there is enough food for every person to have an adequate diet, but that one billion people consume more grain than the other three billion combined. Hunger and starvation are a way of life for over five hundred million people, and many more would be happier and could make a positive impact on society with more variety in their diets. Furthermore, one-half of the child deaths in the world each year are linked to malnutrition.

We do not know how many people have died of starvation throughout the ages, but we do know that there have been thousands of famines. In two thousand years there have been almost that many famines in China alone. Whole villages starved during the African drought of the mid-twentieth century, and famines resulting from war have taken innumerable lives in Biafra, Bangladesh, and Cambodia. Human suffering in such circumstances stretches the imaginations of most North Americans. The real tragedy is that this human suffering need not be, since United Nations studies clearly show that there is enough food for all of Earth's four billion people to have an adequate diet.

The world food situation is critical, complex, and precarious. It is precarious because of decisions made in both wealthy and poor countries on both personal and institutional levels. When enough people make decisions in a broad time and space framework, in service to humanity, and in response to God's call to do the works of justice, we can change this precarious situation.

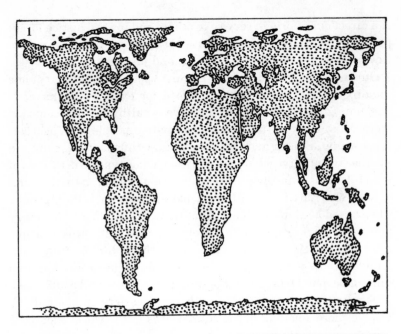

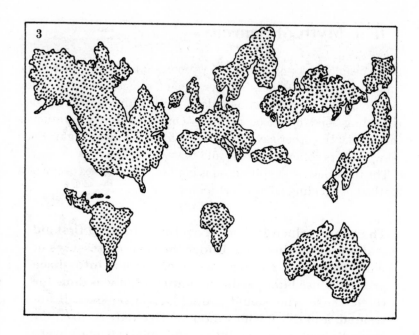

THREE WAYS OF MAPPING THE WORLD. If you look at the map on your wall or in your atlas—or at maps commonly used in textbooks—they will most likely be based on the projection of Gerhard Kremer, known as "Mercator," whose view of the world in 1569 has remained the popular image for more than four hundred years. In Mercator's time Europe was the center of the world. People were mainly concerned with European and Christian interests, and it seemed natural that the world should be centered on the Mediterranean and on Jerusalem. Moreover, Mercator's map is still the best one for plotting direction and for adding up distances.

The three maps on these pages may seem strange to you at first because they are meant to represent different views of the world than Mercator's, which was drawn from the point of view of European navigators. The map designed by Dr. Arno Peters (1) is meant to give a fairer impression of the size of the various continents. You will notice on his "North and South Map" that the southern continents are much larger than on other maps we use. The next two maps demonstrate how we can use mappings of the world in order to show relative population size (2) and wealth (3) (Sources: Peters Projection, World Bank).

1 The Myth of Scarcity

Some people see hunger and starvation as a necessary part of the human condition. Others see permanent hunger and starvation as intolerable. Here are two fundamentally different perspectives regarding the world food problem. One says that starvation is inevitable; the other says that food is a basic human right. Each view leads to different career and lifestyle decisions.

The first view, that starvation is inevitable, endorses *triage* as a method of deciding who will starve.

The triage principle came from the battlefield first aid stations of World War I. Under the severe pressures of war, wounded soldiers were classified into three groups: those likely to die no matter what was done for them, those who would probably recover even if untreated, and those who would survive only if cared for immediately. Since supplies and medical staff were limited, the third group alone received attention. This kind of selective division and care is triage.

Triage is also called "the lifeboat theory." Thus, the world is compared to a lifeboat where only a limited number of people can stay afloat. To invite others aboard courts disaster for everyone in the boat.

Those who opt for triage argue that there is not enough food to go around, so some people, even large numbers, will have to starve. Therefore, they say, countries should be divided: some should eat and some should starve. This perspective says that human decisions and actions, both personal and collective, are ultimately futile attempts to ward off hunger and starvation.

Many people reject triage or the lifeboat theory. They say that we can and must provide adequate food for every person. This leads us to examine the second perspective, that food is a basic human right.

The right to food is rooted in the intrinsic value of human life. It is based on the fact that the resources of the Earth belong to the whole human family, that the whole human family is together in the lifeboat. For Christians, the right to food is also rooted in Jesus' compassionate concern for people on the fringes of society without basic necessities, and in the mystery of his identification with people in need—"I was hungry and you gave me food; I was thirsty and you gave me drink" (Matthew 25:35).

The need for food and the gnawing pain of permanent hunger violates human life and thwarts full human development. A nutritionally adequate diet promotes human life and full development. To provide everyone with such a diet, Earth's food-producing resources must not be exploited by those in power, but be managed wisely for the benefit of everyone. The United States Congress recognized that fact when it responded to public concern and stated that the basic human right to food will be a fundamental point of reference in the formulation of U.S. policy in all areas which bear on hunger.

Our personal and collective decisions can move us firmly and steadily toward the day when wise management of resources assures everyone of a nutritionally adequate diet. Accomplishing such a task calls for creativity, courage, and hard work on personal and collective levels. It calls for imagineers with a wide variety of talents working in a wide variety of careers. To see the problem in better perspective, we should examine the balance between people's needs and Earth's food-producing resources.

2 Earth's Balance Sheet

Four conditions directly affect the amount of food actually available to people: (1) physical resources of land and water, (2) control of those physical resources, (3) demand for food in both quantity and quality, and (4) distribution of food. Each of these conditions can help or hinder the balancing of people's needs with Earth's resources.

LAND AND WATER

Physical resources of land and water are essential to food production. According to conventional agriculture, land can be used in two ways to increase the food supply: expand the area under cultivation, or increase the yield on land already cultivated. The first approach, *extensive land use,* has been used from the dawn of the agricultural age. The second approach, *intensive land use,* has become popular with the pressure of increasing population. This shift to more intensive use of land, however, has not been worldwide since it demands increased amounts of water, energy, fertilizer, and pesticides. Poor countries cannot afford these resources and are therefore thwarted in their efforts toward more intensive land use. Water irrigates land and provides fish, which is an important source of food and nutrition for many people. Intensive fishing could significantly increase this source of food.

CONTROL OF RESOURCES

Control over food-producing resources is a second condition which directly affects the amount of food actually available to people. When a minority of people controls the majority of agricultural land, the imbalance between people's needs and the use of that land is compounded. For example, in certain parts of Mexico, commercial farmers produce tomatoes for Americans instead of corn for Mexicans because they can make more money. In Colombia, the handful of wealthy landowners who control about seventy percent of the land grow flowers for export instead of wheat for local consumption because they can make more money. And in Pakistan, commercial growers produce corn to be converted into sweetener for soft drinks and other luxury processed foods instead of growing food for needy people, because they too can make more money. In the United States, some farmers have been paid not to plant all their fields, while others have been subsidized for growing non-essentials like tobacco. The cumulative effect of all these decisions is to decrease significantly the

Norman Borlaug
Plant Pathologist and Geneticist
Awarded Nobel Peace Prize—1970

October 21, 1970, began like any other day in the life of Norman Borlaug. Tanned, dusty, sweaty, and knee-high in an experimental wheat crop about fifty miles outside Mexico City, he was surprised by a visit from his excited wife, Margaret. She brought good news—Borlaug had been selected for the Nobel Peace Prize for his leadership in the worldwide effort to increase food production. Somewhat typically he pushed his hat back, grinned, and replied, "That's just fine, but I still have a day's work to do here. After that we'll celebrate."

Borlaug and his co-workers first went to Mexico in 1944 at the invitation of the government. Their task was to "export the U.S. agricultural revolution to Mexico." To accomplish that revolution, one of their primary goals was the improvement of the tall, thin-stemmed varieties of Mexican wheat.

Borlaug's team approached their work with vigor and dedication. Instead of growing one experimental crop each year, they grew two alternative crops each year at different sites. Their aggressive action paid off in the development of high-yield, highly adaptable dwarf wheats, and the "Green Revolution" was on its way.

The son of Norwegian immigrants to America, Borlaug grew up on a farm near Cresco, Iowa. He probably would have remained there except that his grandfather constantly urged him to go to college. Like many of today's students, Borlaug worked his way through school. He earned a bachelor's degree in forestry from the University of Minnesota and four years later a doctorate in plant pathology from the same university.

Despite his international acclaim, Norman Borlaug takes a cautious view of the ultimate benefit of his work to society. As he sees it, unless population growth is checked, his work and that of his fellow scientists is only a temporary truce in the war against hunger and deprivation. Where do we stand in this battle?

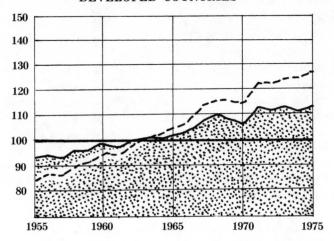

DEVELOPED COUNTRIES

SHADED AREA: PER CAPITA FOOD PRODUCTION
BROKEN LINE: TOTAL FOOD PRODUCTION

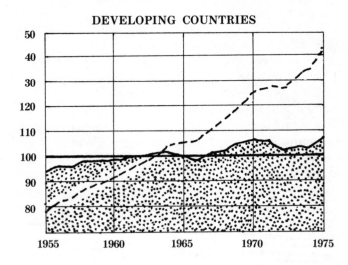

DEVELOPING COUNTRIES

TOTAL AND PER CAPITA FOOD PRODUCTION IN DEVELOPED AND DEVELOPING COUNTRIES, 1955-1975. This figure illustrates that despite an increase in food production worldwide, per capita production in developing countries has not risen proportionately (Source: Sewell, et. al.).

amount of food actually available to people. Until agriculture becomes, first and foremost, a way for people to produce the food they need, the small minority who controls the majority of agricultural land decides *who* shall eat, *if* they shall eat, and *what* they shall eat.

DEMAND FOR FOOD

The escalating demand for food is a third condition which directly affects food availability. As the number of people increases, the *quantity* of food demanded also increases. As eating habits become more affluent, the *quality* of food demanded changes. When population increases faster than food production, the amount of food available to each person declines. Over a recent fifteen year period, food production in both developed and developing countries increased rather consistently, but the amount of food actually available to each person in poor countries did not parallel the total increase. In wealthy countries, however, the amount of food available to each person increased significantly.

Demand for food—both in quantity and quality—will continue to rise. Nutrition experts and economists point out these startling facts:

The same amount of food that feeds one million Americans today could feed over seven million Chinese on a traditional Chinese diet. People in wealthy nations use practically as much cereal to feed their animals as people in poor countries use as food for themselves. It takes roughly five times as much land, water, and fertilizer to support an average North American as it does an average Indian, Nigerian, or Colombian.

FOOD DISTRIBUTION SYSTEMS

Food distribution systems is a fourth condition which directly affects how much food is actually available to people. Studies show that there is sufficient food to go around, but that not enough of it is distributed to those in need. Complex systems of land control and distribution decisions compound the problem. Both among countries and within them, those who can pay for it claim a disproportionate share of food.

Thus, we see that the balance between people's needs and Earth's food-producing resources is definitely out of kilter. This unfortunate and unjust situation does not have to continue. It is not inevitable that some people starve while others destroy or waste food. It is not inevitable that some people scratch out a bare subsistence while others live in ways that actively reduce Earth's food-growing capacity. Clearly, our personal and collective career and lifestyle decisions can effect change. As Christians, stewards of God's gift of creation, we can make career and lifestyle choices that make a positive impact on society and shape a just society. Thus we hasten the day when all people can enjoy a nutritionally adequate diet.

When we understand the conditions which directly affect how much food is actually available to people, we have the information we need to make wise, effective decisions. Interpreting that information as thoroughly and objectively as possible within a broad framework prepares us to choose a course of action, a career and a lifestyle that serve the real needs of people and direct this world toward justice.

3 The Other Side of the Chasm

Experience colors our perceptions. Depending upon where we live in the world—whether in a poor or wealthy country—we tend to see world hunger from a different perspective. For people in poor countries, the late twentieth century is a particularly critical time, since United Nations studies estimate that one out of every four people lives below the lower limit of protein and energy requirements.

Some people say that starvation is inevitable in those poor countries. Leaders in Tanzania, Bangladesh, and China, however, see permanent hunger as intolerable and food as a basic human right.

TANZANIA

In the mid-1970s, Tanzania was one of the five most critically grain-deficient countries in the world. Then President Julius Nyerere and his government set food self-reliance as their primary goal. They promoted research and provided positive incentives to cereal producers. They subsidized fertilizers and offered free advice on the use of improved seed varieties. They discontinued subsidies on animal feed, restricted grain exports, and undertook a special program for the development of maize. Unfortunately, bureaucratic administrators tried to push food self-reliance on the people without their initiative and involvement. Nyerere soon discovered that top-down government order does not work. Unwittingly, it encourages people to become spectators and thus thwarts their potential to make wise and responsible decisions.

BANGLADESH

Like Tanzania, Bangladesh aims at food self-reliance. Despite its rich soil, abundant water and sunshine, rice yields per acre in the mid-1970s were only one-half of the world average. Then the government initiated policies that subsidized prices for fertilizer and pesticides, supplied free irrigation, and gave farm credit easily. Still, production did not increase significantly. The problem is one of *control*. About ninety percent of all the land in Bangladesh is worked by tenants who do not own the land. As long as a minority controls its use, that land is under-utilized and food self-reliance an unrealistic goal.

CHINA

Unlike Tanzania and Bangladesh, China's focus is on *local* food self-reliance. Pre-1949 China was ravaged by hunger, disease, and starvation. Then decisions for extensive land reform paved the way for increased agricultural productivity, and by the early 1960s, there was no shortage of food for that country's nearly one billion people. The Chinese have succeeded in balancing their need for food with their food-producing resources.

Tanzania, Bangladesh, and China illustrate the importance of development decisions on both personal and institutional levels. They illustrate the need for sufficient information and for sound interpretation of that information. In each case, people lined up alternatives and asked, "What would happen if . . . ?" Then they chose a course of action rooted in personal or societal values and consistent with their fundamental perspective. Implementing those decisions brings new information and insights which in turn leads to evaluation and to further decisions.

4 Decisions on an Institutional Level

Disastrous weather conditions in the early seventies contributed to the rapid deterioration of the world food supply. Consequently, hundreds of thousands of men, women, and children died of starvation. The urgency of the situation prompted the United Nations to sponsor a World Food Conference to discuss ways to maintain adequate food supplies and to harness the efforts of all nations to respond to hunger and malnutrition. Delegates from around the world met in Rome and recommended immediate and coordinated action on three important fronts: (1) increase food production, especially in developing countries; (2) improve distribution and consumption of food; (3) build a system of food security. These recommendations have not yet been sufficiently implemented.

The crisis within Cambodia in the late seventies demonstrates how devastating food shortages can become as well as how difficult it is to bring international aid to bear on these national emergencies.

On both sides of the wealthy-poor chasm people are deciding today who shall eat tomorrow. If we want all people to have a nutritionally adequate diet, we can all make some significant decisions. For instance, *people in developing countries* can direct their energies toward land reform, improved credit, marketing, distribution techniques, and cooperative organizations for rural workers. They can intensify rural educational efforts and implement food and nutrition policies to improve the diet for those most vulnerable and deprived.

People in industrialized nations can direct their energies toward major changes in trade, investment, and aid patterns in order to support developing countries' efforts at food self-reliance. We can use our political power to assure that national agricultural policies are sensitive to local producers and consumers as well as to those beyond our national borders. By our collective decisions, we can influence public policy which has important repercussions elsewhere in the world.

United States public policy profoundly affects and largely determines what happens elsewhere in the world. This is due in part to the world's increasing dependence on U.S. grain exports. In 1975, the United States provided over sixty percent of the corn, seventy-five percent of the soybeans, and forty percent of the wheat traded on the world market. It even exported over twenty-five percent of the rice. Public policy decisions determine where those grains go and so count heavily in determining who shall eat.

Asked how people in industrialized nations can help people in countries like his own, Tanzania's President Julius K. Nyerere once responded:

> **The world is organized in such a way that the poor are exploited by the rich. It does not matter how hard we work—how much coffee, cotton, and sisal we produce—the world has a built-in mechanism for exploitation so that we don't get the full benefit of our work. It is taken by the rich. This system has to be deliberately changed by those who have power . . . They must use their influence to educate the general public of their country so that they will stop this exploitation . . . So my message is—agitate and educate—ceaselessly and relentlessly.**

Nyerere says that if we can understand the problems of the poor in our own nation we can understand the problems of the poor of the world. Those problems are compounded when injustice is structured into the institutions of society. Our collective decisions have shaped those institutions, however, and our collective decisions can change them.

5 Decisions That Count

The way we look at hunger in the world is the key to the decisions we make about it. If we see hunger and starvation as inevitable, we will probably base our decisions, perhaps inadvertently, on the principle of triage. If we see hunger as intolerable and food as a basic human right, we will want our personal and collective decisions to assure that right for everyone.

In Cambodia, for example, the collective decisions of many

people have perpetuated war and injustice which in turn have led to widespread starvation. Starvation and poverty can also produce further injustice and perhaps war because people cannot be expected to promote justice and peace for others when they are unable to meet their own needs for basic nutrition and physical security. Inevitably, their viewpoint is narrowed, and survival itself becomes an overriding priority. The *Pastoral Constitution on the Church in the Modern World* of Vatican II attested to this moral priority in strong words:

The Fathers and Doctors of the Church held this view, teaching that people are obliged to come to the relief of the poor and to do so not merely out of their superfluous goods. If a person is in extreme necessity, he has the right to take from the riches of others what he himself needs (#69).

Pope John Paul II repeated this same thought when he told the United Nations assembly that "the spirit of war . . . springs up and grows to maturity where the inalienable rights of people are violated." This strongly worded principle regarding the cause of war can be restated as a peace principle: when basic human rights—the right to food and security—are assured to every human being, then peace will be more fully ensured.

6 Change Agents at Work

Bread for the World, Focus: HOPE, and the Center for Science in the Public Interest are change agents in today's society. Each began with personal decisions of a few concerned people. All have been brought to a social or community level by the collective decisions of many others. All are rooted in the right of all peoples to food, but each works with a different thrust. Together they illustrate a variety of possibilities open to those who ask, "What can I do?"

BREAD FOR THE WORLD

Arthur Simon was a hardworking Lutheran pastor on Manhattan's lower east side when the African drought of the mid-twentieth century came to the world's attention. To him, the reality was shocking. Simon knew all too well the poverty and hunger of his own neighborhood and congregation. That too was shocking. It led Simon and a handful of other Christians to consider what the churches were doing—and not doing—about world hunger. Building on the potential of ordinary people to be change agents, they formed a grassroots citizens' lobby to shape national food priorities and policies. They organized interested citizens along congressional lines and informed them about hunger-related issues through a monthly newsletter. These citizens, in turn, contacted their elected representatives and influenced government policies that affect hungry people. With good reason they call themselves *Bread for the World*. More than any other single group, Bread for the World was responsible for the public concern that led the U.S. Congress to pass resolutions making the right to food a fundamental point of reference in the formation of United States food policy.

FOCUS: HOPE

Like Bread for the World, *Focus: HOPE* began with the decision of several people to face an acute social and moral crisis. Deeply rooted anger had exploded in rebellion that rocked Detroit in the summer of 1967. Shortly after those tension-filled days, the Urban League took an opinion survey of inner city residents which linked the extensive looting of grocery and drug stores to people's perceptions of unfair, discriminatory treatment. But there was insufficient reliable evidence to support that perception.

Meanwhile, William Cunningham and Jerome Fraser, Catholic priests, were teaching in Detroit. Eleanor Josaitis, mother of five children, was living in a nearby suburban community. United in their determination to understand and to respond to what was happening around them, they organized a massive comparison shopping survey of over 500 food stores and 150 pharmacies. They found conclusive evidence that inner city residents were paying five percent more than their suburban counterparts for the same food from the same supermarket chain. They were paying twenty percent more at the large independents and up to thirty-five percent more at the small corner groceries.

That survey was the beginning of Focus: HOPE's many efforts to combine practical action and education. People at Focus: HOPE saw a need and began a nutritional health program for mothers, infants, and pre-school children in Detroit. Its Food Prescription Program provides food from the U. S. Department of Agriculture to low income mothers and children on a monthly basis, without charge. Over 35,000 mothers and children in Detroit benefit from foods specially selected to offset the health hazards of chronic hunger. They come to the food distribution center with a sense of dignity and self-worth and choose from a variety of meats, juices, and vegetables what is prescribed for their families. The Detroit program has proven so successful that other cities across the country are beginning similar programs to benefit hungry people.

What began with a decision by a few people has

Eleanor Josaitis
Civil Rights Activist

A single event forever marks the life of this energetic woman with warm blue eyes and a ready smile. Eleanor tells it in her own words:

> I remember watching a TV show on the Nuremburg trials and having the movie interrupted with the news story of the riot in Selma, Alabama. I sat in horror watching the police horses ride over the marching people and wondered, "Dear God, is this the United States or Nazi Germany?" I remember sharing my feelings of shock with family and friends and getting the blank expression and comments of "Why be so upset?" At that moment my life took a turn. I read everything I could get my hands on, to try to understand . . .

Reading was only the beginning. Decision and action followed. That summer, Eleanor and her husband sold their suburban ranch-style home and moved with their five children into a large house in an integrated Detroit neighborhood. It was not an easy move. Riots a year earlier had left the city a legacy of tension and fear.

Undaunted, Eleanor joined with Father William Cunningham and developed an organization of volunteers known as Focus: HOPE. A decade later she was the force behind a program that was providing nutritious food each month to over 35,000 poverty-level Detroit mothers and children.

Josaitis combines career and lifestyle in an extraordinary way. Her life is built on faith and the conviction that human decisions and actions make God's presence active in the world. In the strength of that conviction she chaired the City of Detroit's Task Force on Hunger and Malnutrition, published a major booklet on "How to Feed the Hungry" and serves on the National Advisory Committee on Maternal, Infant and Fetal Nutrition.

Eleanor's concern for people and their well-being permeates her home and family life. Their move to the city has given them all a broader vision.

grown to involve more than 22,000 metropolitan Detroit volunteers. What began as the dream of a few has become the goal of many. Imagineers at Focus: HOPE are changing patterns and moving society firmly and steadily toward justice.

THE CENTER FOR SCIENCE IN THE PUBLIC INTEREST

The *Center for Science in the Public Interest* is another way to do the works of justice and to effect change. This Washington-based group provides the public with interesting and understandable information about food, the food industry, and government regulation of food. CSPI initiated and sponsored National Food Days which resulted in local teach-ins at high schools and colleges, educational programs on domestic and world hunger as well as anti-junk-food campaigns.

CSPI echoes President Nyerere's plea to "agitate and educate." Its workers follow and attempt to influence the actions of federal agencies that oversee food safety and nutrition. The Center has initiated legal actions to ban unsafe and poorly tested food additives; petitioned federal agencies for better labeling; and published "how-to" manuals to improve school lunch programs, vended food, and community food policies. CSPI has also inspired citizens' groups across the country to make their voices heard in shaping food policy.

7 Small Steps to Solve Big Problems

We can all be involved, directly or indirectly, in shaping U.S. food policy. Our decisions can reinforce the status quo or they can help to create a climate for change and effect that change. If our perspective is narrow, we will probably opt for business as usual.

If our vision is broad, we will see that our personal decisions can exert a positive influence on food policy. For instance, some of us can and will choose careers with agencies or institutions that directly work on the problem of hunger. All of us can adopt lifestyles that lessen the difficulty of that task.

Before Norman Borlaug and his co-workers produced the Green Revolution, they had to study and prepare themselves. For some, that meant earning academic degrees in biology, chemistry, physics, ecology, or agriculture. For others, it meant learning skills in farming, research, and record-keeping. It meant self-discipline and hard work. Careers that directly work on the problem of hunger must be prepared for with appropriate knowledge and skills.

Highly educated and skilled people are not the only ones whose decisions can direct Earth's resources to meet people's need for a nutritionally adequate diet. Each of us has talents that we can apply to the problem of hunger and different opportunities to use those talents. The needs we encounter often tap unrecognized talents. A few examples illustrate how a diversity of needs taps a diversity of talents.

TANZANIA

For centuries, Tanzania's arid land challenged even the most enterprising farmer. Wells were few; water was a luxury. Then George Cotter developed his own technique for digging wells. Soon over fifty wells were operating and more than 10,000 Tanzanians could work their land with renewed energy and enthusiasm.

UPPER VOLTA

Farmers in the Yatenga District of Upper Volta could not tap the nearby Black and White Volta Rivers to irrigate their parched land. Then Mamadou and his son organized other local farmers to construct drainage basins and small dams. More land was cultivated and used for a longer season, enabling them to feed their families nutritiously with a more varied diet.

THE UNITED STATES

Martha Norman realized that her sons were growing up hooked on the junk-foods advertised on television. She decided to counter that impact by feeding them more fresh fruits and vegetables. Supermarket prices were high and the quality low, so Martha and two friends began to purchase produce from the farmer's market. Their cooperative venture grew and soon involved more than forty families. People were eating higher quality food for a lower price.

In the Chicago area the problem of high food prices was compounded by distribution costs. Then Paul Horvat formed direct farmer-consumer links by organizing more than 200 buying clubs serving nearly 45,000 people. Both small-scale farmers and low-income, inner city residents benefited from Horvat's efforts.

Students at Wayne State University seemed unconcerned about hunger in their city. To alert them to the problem, members of Wayne's Food Task Force decided to enlist the help of several dance students. They organized a campus-wide Food Day where hundreds of students watched Anita Surma and Andrzej Rozecki dramatize hunger's unrelenting pursuit of her unwilling prey. Some of the students in the audience later became involved in hunger-related projects.

These are all small steps. Enough small steps taken by enough concerned people can make a big difference, however. Our personal and collective decisions can move us firmly and steadily toward the day when every person on this Earth has the food that is necessary for full human life.

These decisions can be costly. Christians are offered a poignant reminder of the cost of full human life every time we gather to celebrate Eucharist. Because one man was willing to lay down his life, all people can know the fullness of life. Because one man offered himself as bread to be broken, all people who experience brokenness can be made whole. Every time we gather in Jesus' name to break the Bread of his Body and drink from the Cup of his Blood, we are challenged anew and gifted with the ability to base our lives in love and direct them toward justice. In response to the hunger crisis of this century some of us can choose careers that work to achieve a balance between people's needs and Earth's food-producing resources. All of us can choose lifestyles that promote sharing of those resources and the development of full human life.

REVIEW QUESTIONS

1) What is the real tragedy in the world food situation?

2) On what grounds do many people believe that food is a basic human right? Why do some people believe in triage?

3) What are the four conditions which directly affect the amount of food available? How do our personal and collective decisions in turn affect those conditions?

4) How do Tanzania, Bangladesh, and China illustrate the importance of development decisions on both personal and institutional levels?

5) What can people in developing countries do to increase the food supply in their own countries? What can people in industrialized nations do to enhance those efforts?

6) Why do United States citizens have a big responsibility for the world food situation? How can we get involved in shaping national food policy?

7) How can collective decisions perpetuate starvation, poverty, and war?

8) How do agencies such as Bread for the World, Focus: HOPE, and the Center for Science in the Public Interest develop and affect society?

9) What are some career and lifestyle decisions involving the food issue that could move the world toward justice?

7

Energy:
Powering Planet Earth

Energy is
for the mechanical world
what consciousness is
for the human world.

If energy fails,
everything fails.

E. F. Schumacher

Our world moves on energy. Energy from natural resources such as oil, coal, and natural gas powers the technological society in which we live. The use of these resources requires wisdom and care. Many people take energy and our natural resources for granted, and many more find it difficult to grasp the worldwide consequences of energy policy.

An old Hindu fable illustrates the problem. It describes six blind but intellectually curious men attempting to understand and describe an elephant. Each man touched a different part of the large animal and so reached a different understanding of "elephant." One felt its broad side and likened the elephant to a wall. Another felt its tusk and concluded that an elephant was like a spear. Its squirming trunk convinced the third man that an elephant was snakelike, while its huge, round leg made the fourth man think that an elephant must be like a tree. The fifth man touched its ear and decided that an elephant was like a fan. The last man held its tail and described the elephant as being like a rope.

This story demonstrates how insufficient information can comically distort perception. Decisions based on distorted perception can be counterproductive and even disastrous. Fortunately, the blind men in the fable did not have to make decisions based on their understanding of "elephant." We, however, *do* have to make decisions—major decisions—based on our understanding of "energy." We can make these decisions wisely when we gather as much accurate information as possible and when we interpret that information within a broad framework. We *will* make decisions; we can make *wise* decisions if we understand the realities of energy.

1 Stored Sunshine

Coal, oil, and natural gas are precious reserves of stored sunshine. These fossil fuels light and heat our homes and public buildings, power our machines, and fuel our automobiles and jet planes. They are vital to the industrial muscle of developed nations.

Many estimates have been made concerning the life expectancy of these fossil fuels. However optimistic or pessimistic, all estimates agree that we cannot rely indefinitely on cheap and abundant fossil fuels as our prime source of energy. Their inexhaustibility is a myth. This myth has uncanny power to distort our perception and lull us into ways of being and doing that are counterproductive and even disastrous.

People in the past discovered the potential energy of fossil fuels and developed the technology to utilize that potential. Our challenge in the present is to discover *new* energy sources and develop technology to power a planet that for over one hundred years has relied increasingly on fossil fuels. We need to examine present energy use, weigh alternate possibilities, and direct society's institutions toward those possibilities by wise decisions and skillful use of talents. Career decisions of some of us will help determine what our new energy sources will be. The lifestyle decisions of all of us will determine how those sources will be used.

Energy use can fit into the four broad periods of history previously described:

1) **before the discovery of agriculture.**

2) **from the discovery of agriculture to the beginning of the Industrial Revolution.**

3) **from the Industrial Revolution to World War II.**

4) **from World War II to the present.**

1) **Before people discovered agriculture, they lived by hunting, fishing, and gathering wild fruits.** Muscle power was their primary energy source. That first historical period was very long, involving millions of years.

2) **In the second period, people learned to use fire and wind, to domesticate animals, and to grow food.** Then they were able to decrease their use of muscle power as a primary energy source and to harness energy from the environment. Energy sources were mostly natural and renewable—water, wind, and plants. The tempo of that long agricultural age quickened in response to the interplay of supply and demand, and the decisions of enterprising, imagineering people. In the late eighteenth century, this tempo accelerated noticeably. Industry gained a foothold, and dependence on water, wind, and plants for energy gave way to dependence on other resources such as coal, gas, and petroleum. Thus, the third period of history was ushered in by an energy revolution.

3) **Industrialization, accompanied by an upsurge in the use of fossil fuels, made possible the transition from an agrarian or farming economy to a more modern, industrialized economy.** Population increased. People flocked to cities. Jobs became more skilled. The division of labor was introduced. Mass production became a reality. Innovative men and women made decisions that changed both history and economics. Those decisions and the society they created forever separates the modern from the ancient world.

4) **In our last historical period, from World War II to the present, energy consumption has mushroomed, especially in industrialized nations.** Harnessing nuclear power brought a quantum increase in the amount of energy available from the environment. The decision to use nuclear power to generate electricity has been hailed by some as the answer to dwindling fossil fuel supplies and lamented by others as environmentally irresponsible.

Our decisions in this open-ended fourth period of history will shape our future course. The decisions we make or fail to make today, our career and lifestyle choices, will determine what life in our world will be like tomorrow. Sufficient information about energy resources and adequate understanding of the implications of that information can broaden our vision and lead to decisions that create new and better ways of living and working in this world.

2 Dispelling Energy's Illusions

Industrialized America has long been accustomed to plentiful energy supplies. Our early growth as a nation and our economic base would have been impossible without them. The oil embargo in mid-1973 jolted us. Drivers scrambled to gasoline pumps; homeowners pushed thermostats down; industry curtailed production. The oil embargo threatened the very foundation of our national lifestyle and toppled the time-honored view that abundant, cheap energy was our birthright. There was even talk of war over the control of resources. The embargo forced home the fact that fossil fuels are finite and will not last forever. Coal, oil, and natural gas cannot be used in the future as they have been in the past.

Coal is least scarce among the fossil fuels. In ancient times it was used in small amounts and its use increased steadily from about the fourteenth century. By the nineteenth century, coal had contributed significantly to the Industrial Revolution and by the early part of this century it was providing about eighty percent of the world's energy needs. Then, shortly after World War II, economics brought petroleum to the forefront.

The world's known oil fields are small compared with coal deposits. Nevertheless, by the mid-1960s, **petroleum** had clearly replaced coal as the world's primary energy source. Demand continues to rise, especially in industrialized nations. The United States with only six percent of the world's population, accounted

for nearly thirty percent of the world's petroleum consumption in the late 1970s.

Natural gas ranks lower in known reserves than both coal and oil. Its use causes minimal environmental problems compared with coal and oil, but as the cost of drilling for these resources rises, natural gas becomes less readily available. Thus, as a practical and reliable energy source for the future, its outlook is rather bleak.

Nuclear power is seen by some as the only realistic alternative to a continued dependence on fossil fuels. Supporters claim that widespread use of nuclear power will bring an age of unprecedented clean, cheap, safe, and reliable energy. Critics argue that its widespread use will increase the danger of radioactive pollution of the planet and even threaten the continuance of life itself. Those promoting nuclear power face these mounting concerns:

    1) **the danger that an accident either in a plant or in the transport of radioactive materials could do untold damage to people and to our physical environment;**

158 Energy

2) the danger that as nuclear technology spreads, terrorists or criminal groups will have easier access to nuclear material;

3) the danger that a growing number of countries will be able to produce their own nuclear weapons;

4) the problem that we have not yet found adequate methods to dispose of nuclear waste which retains its killing power for half a million years.

Only rigid security measures, near-perfect technology, and the highest levels of human performance can prevent nuclear byproducts from destroying human lives.

The euphoria and hope that nuclear power would be *the* energy answer for the future has been short-lived. Even after we separate facts from speculation—a necessary step in any sound decision—we must admit that nuclear energy is fraught with ambiguity. Here especially, decisions must be made in a broad framework.

One fact is clear. The era of cheap oil and gas has ended and an energy transition is underway. How our world will look in the future depends on the decisions we make today about energy sources. We can continue to live in ways that feed on the myth of inexhaustibility, or we can face the challenge of seeing beyond energy's illusions.

Perhaps the most common illusion of all is the vague dream that "something will happen" to solve the energy crunch. That "something" will *not* happen without the imagination, decisions, and hard work of *people*. People made the decisions and developed the technology to power this planet by coal, oil, gas, and nuclear energy. People can make the decisions and develop the technology to power this planet by other means. Imagineering can help us to bring human values, technological competence, and a broad perspective to this challenging task. A look at nature's cycle can provide us with important information.

Thornton F. Bradshaw
Industrialist and Civic Leader

Thornton Bradshaw is a successful business executive with a strong sense of corporate social responsibility. When he was elected president of Atlantic Richfield Company in 1964, roughly fifty percent of the American people had lost confidence in the leaders of major corporations. Fifteen years later, that figure had jumped to about eighty percent as business leaders became the battered targets of a discouraged and disillusioned public.

In the midst of growing turmoil, Bradshaw struggled to make ARCO a successful and socially responsible corporate citizen. On more than one occasion he broke ranks and even shocked the rest of the oil industry with what appeared to be "heretical" positions.

Bradshaw surprised a lot of people in the late 1970s when he openly supported a tax on oil companys' excess profits and the repeal of the oil depletion allowance. He surprised a lot more when he mounted a national campaign to raise consciousness on the subject of mass transit, a competitive form of transportation in which ARCO has no financial stake. Indeed, under Bradshaw's leadership, ARCO's position on the environment and other industrial rallying points often seemed to go against the current.

Bradshaw was educated at Harvard, taught at Harvard Business School, and was partner in a management consulting firm before moving to Atlantic Richfield. His strong sense of social responsibility permeates his involvement in civic projects such as the Los Angeles Philharmonic Association, the Performing Arts Council of Los Angeles, and the Aspen Institute for Humanistic Studies. That same sense of social responsibility permeates Bradshaw's decisions at ARCO where no decision is made without first considering its social and political implications. According to Bradshaw, "Our lives are thus made far more difficult, more troubled, frequently more concerned—and yet infinitely richer in a very human sense. I would make that bargain any time."

3 Tapping Nature's Cycle

Water power, wind power, plant power, and direct sunlight are renewable sources of energy. Because they tap nature's cycle, they are relatively inexhaustible. When we develop the technological expertise to make their widespread use possible and economically advantageous, we can supply our planet's entire energy needs. To do that—to tap nature's cycle to power the needs of industrial society—may well be the greatest challenge of our century.

Imaginative, enterprising men and women in past ages developed techniques for using water and wind power to harness energy from the environment and so lessen their own physical labor. They used water power directly to spin the wheels that pumped water and ground grain. They used wind power to grind and thresh grain, cut wood, and pump water. Human muscle and animal power were small compared with the energy that could be generated from naturally occurring resources of water and wind.

Water and wind energy use continues in our own day. Water power is used to power even large-scale hydro-electric sites. Windmills are still being used and people are developing technology for economic applications. For example, in Denmark recently, people built a 2,000-kilowatt wind turbine to generate power for a college.

Plant power is another source of renewable energy. The huge amounts of organic matter which the Earth produces each year are plant power, called biomass. When we burn wood, for example, we are using biomass. Open burning of wood and leaves is the best known, but probably the least efficient, way to use plant power. Decomposing organic matter under the right conditions, however, can convert "waste" into energy. Many developing countries use biomass conversion to produce fuel for cooking and lighting. Industrialized nations have more waste to burn. Some large industrial cities have recently begun to utilize their garbage to produce energy.

Sun power is the source of all our mechanical energy. Without the exploding atoms at the sun's center, there would be no wind or water power, no organic material to decompose, no stored sunshine of fossil fuels. We can harness the sun itself as a mechanical source of energy. This is *solar* energy, a non-polluting, limitless source of energy, that offers great potential for meeting Earth's energy needs both now and in the future. For the eighty percent of the world's people who live in poor countries within thirty-five degrees of the equator, technological and economic advances in the development of solar energy could mean the difference between lives of misery and lives of promise.

Technology—**brain power**—is now available to tap nature's cycle for solar energy. Expanding its use from small decentralized installations to broad-scale commercial use on an economically acceptable scale remains a major challenge. Personal and collective decisions are needed to orient research in that direction and to implement that research in service and toward justice. This is a task that demands our best efforts.

4 Disparity's New Face

By the early 1900s, world energy consumption was concentrated among a limited group of countries. Today it is only slightly less concentrated. According to the following chart, North America, Europe, and the Soviet Union comprise about twenty-four percent of the world's population, but consume approximately seventy-eight percent of the world's energy. The balance of the world's population (seventy-six percent) uses only twenty-two percent of the world's energy.

Most poor countries are also energy poor. They have neither fossil fuel reserves nor financial resources. Human and animal muscle power are inadequate to support their development efforts. They need a secure and reliable supply of low-cost energy, but rising prices for fuel, grain, fertilizer, and manufactured goods seems to be their lot. Disparity's "new face" is hauntingly familiar.

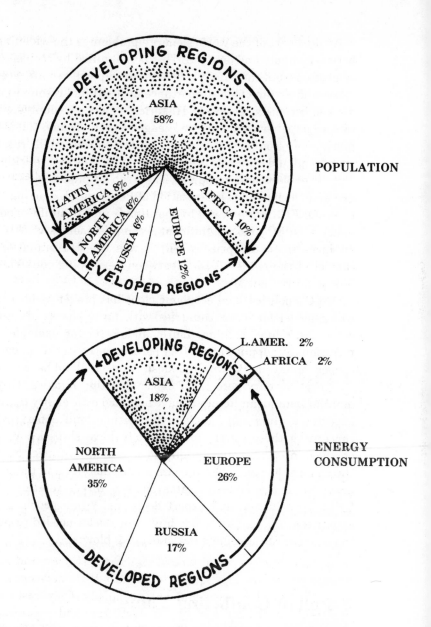

POPULATION

ENERGY CONSUMPTION

POPULATION AND ENERGY CONSUMPTION COMPARED
(Source: United Nations).

At the heart of the world's energy problem is the widening gap between supply and demand. This is magnified by economic considerations, but the supply and demand gap will remain a central cause and assume more importance as fossil fuel resources dwindle and become more costly. Historically, when a country wanted to buy, supplier countries were eager to sell. Today, the issue is much more complex. Countries with non renewable resources such as oil and minerals are asking themselves how quickly they want to exploit those resources. The Arab oil-producing states, for example, formed the Organization of Petroleum Exporting Countries (OPEC) in an effort to coordinate and to unify exporting policies. OPEC's most significant accomplishment was more than an increase in the price of oil; it was the determination and control of the *terms of trade* between developing countries and industrialized nations.

OPEC's political and economic clout has proven to be a tantalizing model for other countries with large shares of valuable resources. Chile, Zambia, Zaire, and Peru, for example, have traditionally supplied about fifty percent of the world's exportable copper. Malaysia, Bolivia, Indonesia, and Thailand have supplied well over seventy percent of exportable tin; Jamaica, Guyana, and the Dominican Republic have supplied over eighty percent of exportable aluminum. Collective decisions and export policies concerning these commodities already have shifted power and changed international relations. People in all countries have felt the change. For example, the size of automobiles and the price of gasoline in the United States show a direct relationship to OPEC's production and export decisions. When people in poor countries cannot afford to pay higher prices for needed resources, the squeeze can become a death-dealing blow.

5 Pull of Conflicting Values

When Maslow described his hierarchy, he described it as one of needs. In another sense, it is a hierarchy of values, since needs and values are closely linked. A person who is always hungry, for example, places a higher value on alleviating hunger than on giving and receiving affection. A person who is habitually fearful and anxious values security more than self-actualization. Societies are like that too. When food and safety are a people's primary needs, they are highly valued. They become dominating elements in those people's decisions.

Needs and values in poor countries differ from those in rich ones. From both sides of the chasm people look at the same energy picture but judge it differently because of different needs and values. Those needs and related values are reflected in the way that people live, in their lifestyles and careers.

In the mid-1970s, a typical worker in Bolivia or Bangladesh was spending nearly eighty percent of his meager income to feed his family. As the cost of importing petroleum-based fertilizer goes up, it becomes less available and grain becomes more precious. As food prices increase, this family may join the five hundred million people who face hunger and starvation in their daily lives.

At the same time, a typical worker in the United States was spending roughly fifteen to twenty percent of his or her income on food and another five to ten percent on gasoline and other fuels. As the cost of food and fuel rises, Americans pay higher prices. Economic conditions of supply and demand are at work here, but American incomes are such that, whatever the increase, many Americans can pay.

Despite its cost, North Americans are using energy resources as fast as ever. Looking at the world in a broad framework, the question looms large: Can the world afford a United States? It is a question of values and ultimately of justice. Just as U.S. food policy recognizes the right of all people to a nutritionally adequate diet, so too U.S. energy policy must recognize the right of all people to the world's energy resources.

6 Beyond a Fossil Energy Policy

Industrialization has made possible an adequate level of amenities for most North Americans and lives of comfort and affluence for many. Our energy-intensive lifestyles evolved when coal, oil, and other resources were abundant. They seemed unlimited. Today, we know they *are* limited. Today, from a broader perspective we can examine the personal and collective decisions and the policies that used those resources so freely. We must evaluate their effectiveness and their energy-efficiency, using the data we gather to make decisions that will create viable possibilities for future generations.

7 Trimming the Fat

Lifestyles in the United States and in West Germany are modern and, in many ways, similar. However, a recent comparison of two suburban families in those countries shows that, on the average, citizens of the United States consume energy at twice the rate as do their counterparts in West Germany. Despite their similarities, there are some significant differences.

HINSDALE

Hinsdale, Illinois, is home for many corporate executives and their families. In the past, they drove to work in Chicago in large, gas-guzzling cars. Now they crowd into the commuter train each day for the fifty-mile round trip. Since Hinsdale has no public transportation, a typical mother drives up to 8,000 miles per year just shuttling children to and from scout meetings, dance classes, music lessons, and other activities. Most Hinsdale families have two or more cars, large uninsulated homes, air conditioners, and kitchens with every conceivable energy-using appliance.

ROSRATH

Meanwhile, in Rosrath, West Germany, middle-management executives live with their families in comparable comfort. They too commute to work. Most of them drive the twelve miles to Cologne in gas-sipping compact cars. Many form car pools, enabling them to share their one car with other family members. Children walk or ride bicycles to school, and shoppers bike to conveniently located areas for groceries and other necessities. Most homes are of stone or brick with small windows and heavy doors. There are no air conditioners. Families in Rosrath have many of the modern appliances as do those in Hinsdale, but they use them more efficiently. They have chosen a less wasteful style of life.

Energy waste, or certainly lack of energy conservation, is common in our society. Until recently, many Americans never questioned insufficient insulation of homes and public buildings, inefficient appliances and equipment, and wasteful energy consumption of large, gas-guzzling automobiles and campers. Until recently, there was little talk and less action directed toward recycling paper, aluminum, glass, and other manufactured goods. One energy researcher said flatly, "The largest, cheapest, and most secure near-term source of energy available to the United States is the one-half of our energy budget currently being wasted."

Some people confuse conservation with curtailment. They are afraid that energy conservation will drastically limit human activity, that it will lower living standards and stunt economic growth. But, as the following figure illustrates, conservation need not be curtailment.

Most experts agree that conservation alone is not the long-term answer to this planet's energy dilemma. However, by trimming the fat in our energy consumption now, we can buy the time

WASTE	CONSERVATION	CURTAILMENT
10 mile-per-gallon status symbols	40 mile-per-gallon cars	No private cars
Large, uninsulated homes	Well-insulated houses with efficient heating systems	Cold houses
Inefficient shipping of goods by truck and plane	Efficient railroads for long haul freight	No interstate transport

WASTE, CONSERVATION, AND CURTAILMENT COMPARED
(Adapted from the *New York Times*).

necessary to develop alternate, reliable energy sources that can power planet Earth into the twenty-first century and beyond. We can all contribute to this project by our career and lifestyle decisions.

8 Decision-Making for the Future

Thirteen hundred students at Our Lady of Mercy High School in Farmington, Michigan, are learning to make decisions within a broad perspective. Several years ago, the school's administrators took the initiative and involved faculty, students, and their parents in formulating a philosophy based on shared decision-making. Since that time, school life has assumed a new vibrancy and challenge. Students, faculty, and administrators serve on numerous committees to create and maintain an environment conducive to growth and learning. Together they experience the joys and anguish, the real struggle, of making sound, effective decisions. Together they seek ways to serve human needs and to promote justice.

Hazel Henderson
Social Critic and Economic Advisor

Hazel Henderson, independent futurist, author, lecturer, and civic activist, is in the forefront of a growing number of thinkers increasingly critical of today's leading economists. At a time when the American economy is undergoing strong pressures for change, she is a breath of fresh air—practical, creative, socially conscious, and hopeful.

Henderson points out that most economists fail to take into account human, social, and environmental factors that do not agree with their theoretical systems. As a result, the enormous social costs that accompany unfettered industrial and technological development go largely unmonitored. It is these social costs that are rising rather than real Gross National Product, but since social costs are *added to* rather than *subtracted from* GNP, the GNP appears to be rising. (Every time there is an automobile accident, the GNP goes up!)

Despite her realism about the seamy side of an economic system which ignores social costs, Henderson is not without hope. She sees more and more people who are coming to recognize the need for consumer and environmental protection, for peace and social justice, and who are creating grass-roots citizens' movements to work toward those ends. Thus, a counter-economy is evolving, one that takes into account social costs and "those human needs that lie beyond the marketplace." To that counter-economy and to the human needs it embodies, Henderson gives her best energies.

English-born and educated, Hazel Henderson is an international woman. She has lectured on almost every continent and written in both academic and popular journals. In 1978, she published a collection of essays, *Creating Alternative Futures,* which offers an ethic of human survival, directed to those who want to make the future better than the present.

Recently, the school began a voluntary energy conservation program. From mid-November to mid-March the school operates on an energy calendar. During those months, students attend classes four days each week instead of five, and make consistent, conscientious efforts to grow in responsible management of energy supplies. On several pre-arranged "bulky sweater days," thermostats are set at sixty degrees. On other days, the temperature level is sixty-eight degrees. An energy committee encourages and facilitates car pooling and sponsors contests to surface energy-saving ideas. They publicize energy savings on a large, centrally located bulletin board.

Results have been impressive. In the first four-month period that the energy calendar was operative, Our Lady of Mercy High School saved enough gas to supply the average yearly needs of twenty-two homes and enough electricity to supply the normal needs of twenty-seven homes for three months.

Evaluation is a way of life at Mercy. Decisions can be changed in light of new evidence. People at Mercy are working to create an environment that allows each person to make choices, to explore alternatives to those choices, and to determine future courses of action based on a broad framework and on personal conviction.

Too few of us live in an environment that is so sensitive to the implications of our personal and collective decisions. Each of us, however, can help to create such an environment. People with diverse talents and backgrounds can use their talents to move us toward justice and full human life for everyone. A few examples illustrate:

Myk Davis is a geophysicist who spends his days scrambling around Indonesian mountains collecting water and rock samples from areas which have known volcanic histories. Davis and his co-workers are looking for potential sources of energy within the Earth itself. They hope to discover the relationship between volcanic systems and geothermic systems.

Marianne Dalton is a homemaker and the mother of three young children. She spends her days caring for them and ever so patiently initiating them into family life. To conserve on energy, Marianne heats only those parts of her home that are actually in use and dresses the children warmly during cold weather. Recently the Dalton's insulated their home and helped several neighbors to do the same.

Albert Fritsch, an organic chemist, spends his days at Appalachia-Science in the Public Interest working on problems of strip mining and the environment. Fritsch recently directed a study which investigated practical ways to use energy efficiently. That study was published and now many well-meaning people benefit from its ingenuity and expertise.

The blind men in our Hindu fable would have been hard-pressed if they had to make even tentative decisions based on their understanding of "elephant." They had insufficient facts and insufficient understanding of the few facts that they had. The first steps toward making a sound decision are to gather and to interpret enough pertinent information. Only then are we able to weigh advantages and disadvantages of possible options, test those options for realism and effectiveness, and choose an appropriate course of action. Choosing is the very core of decision-making, but it would be premature without an adequate understanding of realistic alternatives. Finally, implementing our choice, our decision, by appropriate action, enables us to evaluate that decision in light of its effects. By our decisions we can lessen injustice, violence, and hatred in our world and move us together toward justice, peace, and love.

REVIEW QUESTIONS

1) How has energy use evolved over the four broad periods of history described in the chapter?

2) Describe the various sources providing our energy needs today. What are the advantages and disadvantages of each of them?

3) What are some ways that we can use to tap nature's cycle to provide for future energy needs?

4) What has caused the world situation where twenty-four percent of the population consumes approximately seventy-eight percent of the world's energy? What developing countries are included in this twenty-four percent? How can collective decisions and export policies change this situation?

5) How does the widening gap between supply and demand affect relations between developing countries and industrialized nations?

6) What distorted perceptions have made energy waste common in North American society?

7) Why is the question "Can the world afford a United States?" one of values and ultimately of justice?

8) Why is decision-making such an important part of our efforts toward justice? What are some career and lifestyle decisions that could move us in that direction?

Conclusion

And so it is—invitation and challenge. The journey toward justice demands creativity and courage, perseverance and prayer. A contemporary Spanish poet described it something like this:

> **Everything goes on, and everything remains**
> **but it is our task to move forward,**
> **to go on in the making of new roads,**
> **new ways over the oceans.**
>
> **Pilgrim, your footprints and nothing else**
> **have laid the path,**
> **Pilgrim, there are no roads;**
> **You make roads by walking.**

This book has traced some of the roads made by people who preceeded us in history, and it has indicated some broad guidelines for making roads into the future. Knowing the past can help us to deal more effectively with the present and so to share in the world's making. There are no super-highways, and not even very good road maps. We make the roads by our decisions and actions. We move society toward justice by choosing careers and lifestyles that enhance the quality of life and serve humanity. That is what it means to live as Christians on a small planet.

The future is in our hands. How shall we decide?

Index

Food:
availability: compared with population, 136; conditions affecting, 133-134, 137-138; in developing countries, 133-134, 136-140, 142, 165; in North America, 136-137 (see also Right to food; Triage)
exports, 109
prescription program, 146, 147
Fundamental perspective, 13-22, 24-25, 27-28, 31

God (Yahweh): belief in, 21-22; revealed in Hebrew Scripture, 25; revealed in Jesus of Nazareth, 25-32; reveals his will today, 65-69
Green Revolution, 135, 149
Gross National Product, 122-124, 169
Growth (see Industrialization; Pollution; Population)

Industrialization, 99, 105, 107-116, 155-157, 166
Institutions, 50-52 (see also Decisions: impact of collective)
International trade (world trade), 107-109, 141, 164

Jesus of Nazareth: and justice, 25, 27-28, 31-32; and the rich young man, 44-45; revelation of Yahweh, 25, 27-28; sayings, 9, 25, 35-36, 133
John Paul II, Pope, 144
Justice: and affluence, 104-105, 113-116; and Christianity, 24-25, 27-31, 45, 69, 91-94, 106, 115-116, 133, 138, 143-145, 151, 172-173 (see also Justice in the World); and energy use, 157, 162-168; and fundamental perspective, 15-21; and hunger, 133-134, 136-138, 141-144; and poverty, 100-102; described, 28; roots of, 28; sense of, 28-29, 31 (see also Decisions: based on justice; impact of collective and personal)
Justice in the World, 28, 106, 115-116

Maslow, Abraham, 39-41, 45, 97, 104, 124, 128, 164-165
Mentors, 90-93

Needs: and decision-making, 41-42, 58, 72-73, 100-102, 104-105, 132-133, 164-165; described, 39-40; related to values (see Values: related to needs)

Nuclear power, 12, 156, 158-159

Peace, 143-144
People/Poverty cycle, 100-102
Pollution: decisions to eradicate, 120-121; described, 116-117; human cost, 103; urban, 103, 119
Population growth: and economic development, 100-102; defined, 97; historical survey, 97-100; in developing countries, 100-102; in industrialized nations, 104-105; two perspectives, 97
Poverty (see People/Poverty cycle)
Prayer, 63-65

Quality of life, 122, 124-125

Religious sense: and justice, 24-25, 27-28; authentic and inauthentic expressions, 22, 24; described, 21-22; framework for decision-making, 21, 24-25, 27-28, 31-32
Right to food, 132-133, 142-145

Scripture (see Biblical references)
Small Is Beautiful, cited, 123
Solar energy (see Energy sources: nature's cycle)
Spiritual Exercises of St. Ignatius Loyola, 68-69

Talents: and Christian journey, 35-36, 38-39, 45-47; described, 38; effective use of, (see Decision makers)
Technology, 104-105, 107, 109-116, 156, 161-162
Triage (lifeboat theory), 132, 142

Values: and decision-making, 34, 42-43, 49-50, 52-55, 58-69, 71-74, 76-77, 80-89, 96, 100-106, 109-110, 115-116, 117-122, 124-125, 132-134, 137-146, 148, 151, 162, 164-168, 170-171; cultural, 62, 80-89, 104-105, 132-133, 164-168; described, 42-43; economic, 100, 104-106, 109-110, 115, 117-119, 134, 165 (see also Gross National Product); personal, 42-47; related to needs, 42-49, 97-102, 104-106, 115-116, 122, 124-125, 164-165; religious, described, 63-66, 73-74, 76; ways to discover, 43-45

Vatican II, 28, 143 (see also Church in the Modern World)
Voluntary simplicity, 105-106

War, 143-144

Acknowledgments continued from page 4

I am grateful, too, to Sisters Bernarda Durkin and Pauline Sferrella, and to Fred Wessells for their careful work in typing the manuscript; to Sisters Jeanette Halbach and Palmira Perea, leaders of Our Lady of Victory Missionary Sisters, for their moral support during the long months of writing. Finally, I thank the people at Saint Mary's Press— Brother Damian Steger, FSC, its imaginative president; Steve Markham, FSC; and Stephan Nagel, the editor.

Illustrations
Charts by Elizabeth M. Nelson. Artwork on page 151, "The Last Supper" by Jules Chadel, Mr. and Mrs. Ross W. Sloniker, Collection of Twentieth Century Biblical and Religious Prints, reprinted courtesy of Cincinnati Art Museum. Photos: Department of the Army, page 19; Hugh Huelster, page 43; Jean-Claude LeJeune, pages 21, 95; Fortune Monte, page 33; NASA, pages 2, 173; NC Photos, pages 29, 46, 143, 144; Norman Provost, FSC, pages 9, 53, 57, 64, 76, 79, 88-89, 118, 121, 153; Vernon Sigl, page 127; Sun Oil, page 158; Wallowitch, pages 83, 85; World Bank, page 111.

Grateful acknowledgment is made here for permission to reprint the following copyrighted materials:
Selections from *The Jerusalem Bible.* Copyright 1966 by Darton, Longman & Todd, Ltd. and Doubleday & Company, Inc. Reprinted by permission. Selection from "Footprints in the Ashes of Time" by Mary D. Leakey, in *National Geographic,* April 1979. Selection from *Land of the Spotted Eagle* by Chief Luther Standing Bear. Copyright 1933 by Houghton Miffin Company. Reprinted by permission. Selection from "Back to Methuselah," Act 1, *Complete Plays with Prefaces,* Vol. II. Copyright 1963 by Dodd, Mead, and Company. Reprinted by permission of the Society of Authors on behalf of the Bernard Shaw Estate. Selection from *How Do I Know I'm Doing Right?* by Gerard Sloyan, copyright 1976 by National Office of Confraternity of Christian Doctrine. Used with permission of the copyright owner. Selection from *Letters to a Young Poet* by Rainer Maria Rilke. Trans. M. D. Herter Norton. Copyright 1954 by W. W. Norton & Company. Reprinted by permission. Selection from *The Contrasumers: A Citizens Guide to Resource Conservation* by Albert J. Fritsch. Copyright 1974 by Praeger Publishers. Selection from *To Serve the Devil: Colonials and Sojourners* by Paul Jacobs and Saul Landau with Eve Pell. Copyright 1971 by Random House, Inc. Reprinted by permission. Selection from *Devotions upon Emergent Occasions* by John Donne. Copyright 1959 by University of Michigan Press. Reprinted by permission. Selection from *Small Is Beautiful: Economics As If People Mattered* by E. F. Schumacher. Copyright 1973 by Harper & Row, Inc. Reprinted by permission. Selection from *The Voice of Truth.* Vol. VI. *The Selected Works of Mahatma Gandhi.* Ed. Shirman Narayan. Copyright 1968 by Navajivan Publishing House, Ahmedabad, India. Reprinted by permission. Selection from "Interview: President Julius K. Nyerere of Tanzania," *New Internationalist.* Copyright 1973 by New Internationalist Publications Limited. Reprinted by permission. Selection from "Caminante, son tus huellas" by Antonio Machado. Translated by T. Matt Garr, SJ. Reprinted by permission of Paul G. Schervish, SJ.